SEARCHING

FINDING PURPOSE, LAUGHTER AND DISTRACTION, THROUGH SEARCH AND RESCUE

MOOSE MUTLOW

D0889470

Thank you to my colleagues, employers, friends and family for bearing with me through my involvement with Search and Rescue. It remains an intense distraction rather than a sole focus. Fortunately around the world there is a sturdy group of volunteers whose sole focus is search and rescue. They train on their time, buy their own equipment and answer the call every day to help people they don't know get out of situations they don't want to be in.

I encourage everyone not to take this for granted. Support them financially, volunteer your expertise or become a member. You never know when you might need them.

I dedicate this book to those that go out in the worst weather, face the grim task of cleaning up someonelse's mistake and maintain the optimism that saves lives against impossible odds.

Thank you.

FOREWORD

This collection of stories started as a writing exercise to work through the impacts of dealing too closely with trauma and death. There is a cumulative impact to this type of work that many responders deal with consciously and unconsciously.

It is a collection of stories that have tragedy and laughter. Success and failure. They helped me to process the experiences and better understand how they have changed me.

And continue to impact me.

Search and Rescue work seesaws between the extremes of success and failure. You are never sure how things are going to work out when the initial call comes in with breathless panic. Cell phone calls drop and you wait to get reconnected to establish a fuller picture. Occasionally you have only a location and description - Falls trail, medical.

As the mission proceeds more details fill the gaps. You know when it is fatality so you can slow down and pace yourself on the trail. A cardiac with compressions in progress means speed is everything.

There is stress at every turn. People are relying on you to perform. To have the skills and resources to save a life. And this is probably a misplaced faith. Wilderness changes the rules with its remoteness.

It reduces your options. Fast.

Search and Rescue operations reinforce the limits of what is possible and as a technician, medical provider and responder you are intimately aware of them. Occasionally someone beats the odds but not often. Yet teams still leave with optimistic pragmatism to the challenges that they will face and need to overcome.

There is a seductive magic in this delusion.

And it kept bringing me back.

INTRODUCTION

Yosemite has never been about the place for me.

It feels heretical writing that because so many visitors and residents wax lyrically about their love of the park, the waterfalls, cliffs and landscapes.

At times I am stirred by nature's pulse in the Valley. The winter snowcap on Half Dome, the window rattling force of Yosemite Falls and the soaring hulk of El Cap all have drawn a lingering eye.

However my experience has always been shaped not by the place but what I have been part of. The strange opportunities that crop up and I have been drawn into as a participant or observer.

Once you operate in the space of always saying yes when someone calls you up for help opportunities start to line up. I had to be prepared to do some foot work, be a little inconvenienced. But the return for that was always something to provide reflection or reward.

Saying yes led me to evacuating sedated bears in litters. Racing with lights and sirens through the Valley on the way to a multiple vehicle wreck. Swimming journalists through rapids for a morning TV show. Sitting costumed up as a visiting squire as part of a seasonal theater production at the Awahanee Hotel. Balancing chairs on my chin during a Congressional delegation dinner. Being the head gate judge at one the oldest ski races in the country. Salvaging people's belongings after a major rockfall wiped out Curry Village Cabins. Working on the wild fire that nearly destroyed my home.

In my Yosemite life Search and Rescue has been one of the most consistent elements in the last 20 years. I have worked as a tech carrying litters down trails and picking up pizza at the end of the mission. There have been extended assignments where I have slept in the dirt to stay on station during searches. Midnight races to trailheads to meet parties after fatalities on the crags. In Incident Command I have listened to climbers describe their anchor set up prior to allowing rescuers to ascend their fixed lines. Quietly listened in when Medical Control decides CPR can cease.

There are times where I sat with families as they hear the worst news imaginable and felt the stunned silence as their lives flip forever. Escorted bodies out of the backcountry. Rescued laughing strangers from midstream stranding.

There is a lot to love about the mission driven, single minded focus of SAR operations. Generally there is a beginning, middle and end to the assignment. For me, now ensconced in an administrative job where results might take years to appear, a successful three hour carry out can be supremely satisfying.

An end is achieved.

When multiple calls come in and the resources get staggered and stretched I love the level of adaption displayed. One evening with no other rescuers instantly available I was loaded up with a litter pack as the sole responder up the

Yosemite Falls Trail for a carry out. I was told to get going and that other personnel would catch me up.

Which they did, as promised.

The shared experience of rescue still seduces me around its common goal. A single minded doggedness to pursue the extraction of an injured party, locate a late hiker or resolve a missing person mystery.

The beauty of SAR operations rests in everyone doing their job without distraction to achieve the mission goal. The hasty teams, technical teams, heli-tac crew, all function because of the support from behind. Everyone plays a vital role in the mission, no matter how seemingly distant from the response.

Everyone is focused on the outcome.

The power of SAR is that everyone, in that moment, becomes selfless.

1

INCIDENT COMMAND SYSTEM

The ICS or Incident Command System is a standard model used in emergency management to structure response. It allocates roles and responsibilities with delegated authority under the overall direction of an Incident Commander. Big or small responses use some variant of the basic hierarchy.

~

Incident Commander (IC)

The IC influences everything about the response. If they are stressed out, the SAR team will feel it and get stretched. If the IC maintains a cool calm demeanor the team leave relaxed.

Late night the radio tone went out for the team to assemble at the SAR cache. The team's pagers should be blinking and the calls into the cache should be coming quickly in for assignment.

Nothing happens.

The phone lines remained silent.

The IC requested Dispatch to put out the tone again. It is late. Maybe the team had missed it.

Waiting. Still no response.

Now the IC became frustrated.

After the second tone the IC started making radio calls. Still no response to the tone but he managed to directly phone a SAR team member. The IC started shouting that the team needed to respond immediately. More words.

It was relayed that the team was now on the way to the cache.

The team arrived a little worse for wear. Quickly a member reminded the IC that they had asked for the evening off to have a party.

The IC had said yes.

The party had been in full swing when the call out came in. Pagers were turned off. It was just luck that someone had heard a radio transmission.

There was still a call out to respond to. The IC thought on their feet. Grabbing a breathalyzer kit they proceeded to test the team. Each member blows into the meter. They all blow over the limit to drive.

Some more than others. Peeling those with the high numbers off, the IC is left with a small buzzed team to use.

The IC did a bit more shouting before pushing them out the door to respond. Frustrated by the events of the evening he returns to the radio room to coordinate the response. Hopefully the team will burn off their party fumes on the hike in.

Over the radio the IC requested an update on the team's status. Are they driving? Where are they?

No reply. The IC checked the channel setting and repeats the message.

Again no reply.

What is happening? Where is everyone?

The door opened and a team member walks gingerly in.

The IC fumed and ranted. Why are they still here? What is happening? How useless are they all?

The team member reminded the IC that they all had been breathalyzed. All of them were over the driving limit, so although they might, debatably, be ok hiking a trail, driving a government vehicle should be not on the menu that evening.

The IC returned to the radios.

He needed to find a driver.

PLANNING

Weeks after the disappearance we sat in the cache debating next steps. The river continued to be high but was trending down. No clues had turned up and daily patrols had not spotted anything interesting.

Now the river profile was up on the board. It was stylized view of the river's rough gradient along with defined sections identified for ease of access and technical complexity.

The group started painting in details. Probability of Detection (POD), areas inaccessible due to high flow/steep ground, log jams. People started talking through possibilities. Maybe the body had caught high flow the first day and moved way beyond previously established downstream containment lines.

Alternately maybe it was hooked up in the deeper water, chilling and not gassing up.

Previous recoveries on the stretch were debated. Where was their entry point? What was the flow that day? Rising or

falling? Where were they recovered? Were they midstream
or along the bank?

All it was being brain dumped up on the board. And
slowly a way forward was emerging. The search assignments started to narrow and targeted spots were identified.
The next week's plan was formed.

∼

Operations

The call out was for all available EMT's to get to the
Cache asap. A line of school buses had rear ended each
other. Multiple reported injuries. I turned up and was
pointed towards a rig and told to drive fast. Three others
jumped in.

I was too focussed on driving so delegated the lights and
sirens to the person next to me. Keeping both hands on the
wheel without trying to figure out which button to use
seemed sensible. Previously driving an ambulance through
the Valley I had become frustrated when the clinic did not
replied to my radio calls, only to discover later I had been
using the PA system by accident. That had happened with
no driving pressure so delegating was the best way to make
sure the right buttons got pushed. The radio chatter was all
about the accident. Roads were getting shutdown and traffic
was getting held up. Soon enough, with some radio confirmation, the rig jumped the line of stalled vehicles and was
racing in the empty on coming lane.

The accident was on the north side between the tunnels.
Pulling up close to the scene the line of emergency vehicles
extended well downhill of the incident. Leaving the window
open and keys with the vehicle our team grabbed some gear
and made our way up the road.

Tarps were laid out on the ground with patients in various stages of stabilization. If someone was complaining of neck pain they were down on the tarp with a neck collar preparing to be strapped onto a backboard. There were more than a dozen patients, so many we were running out of backboards.

Deeper into the incident students milled about as teachers tried to have some veneer of control. People had been checked and given a Triage tag. The tag was color coded and gave the rescuers a visual guide to the serious of the individuals injuries. Unfortunately the effectiveness of this system had been nullified by the youngsters propensity to change their status from Green (Minor) to Black (Deceased).

The uninjured were having a good time. The living dead in particular. They were becoming a distraction to the genuinely injured.

A ranger stepped up. She exercised what is popularly known as command presence. It was very effective. Students elected to quickly sit muted on the roadside wall and stop changing their status. I felt like I should sit on the wall too after she finished.

The evacuations began. Ambulances headed down the hill. Some to the helicopter landing zone, most out on the road. Thankfully it turned out all were precautionary with no serious injuries.

The responding team began to clean up and head back to vehicles. My first MCI. Multiple Casualty Incident.

~

LOGISTICS

The witching hour for callouts was late afternoon in the

Spring and Early Summer. Around 4pm the phone calls started coming in for assistance on the trail due to dehydration or twisted ankles.

A late carry out mandated that the litter team be fed upon their return. There were a handful of options to accomplish this. The easiest was to call up the pizza place, time the order to coincide with the teams return and make sure that you bought the right amount.

You had to figure out if the litter team was made up of SAR volunteers, park employees or a mix there of. The time of the call out, distance carried and the weather all influenced how many pizzas you ordered. It was a bit touch and go because you wanted to order enough to satisfy, but not enough to create storage problem. Veggie to pepperoni ingredients had to reflect the teams make up and dietary preferences.

I always got more stressed on the amount and breakdown for the pizza order than the emergency response.

One day sitting by the radios monitoring the teams progress I glanced over and spotted a new memo posted.

The Pizza Matrix.

Some bright spark battling the same indecision I faced had created a table to make the decision easier. It cross-referenced litter team numbers, had a seasonal correction and offered insight into not only the size of the pizza to order but a suggested breakdown on flavors and ingredients.

Suddenly the stress fell away.

This was a three large pepperoni, two medium Veggie and one small Hawaiian pizza call out.

HASTY TEAM - DEF. **usually a small team dispatched immediately to respond to an incident to provide support and information.**

We had been dispatched as a Hasty Team to respond to the report of a car wreck off the side of Southside Drive. The location was not completely clear but jumping into the ambulance the adrenaline was pumping as I pulled out with lights and sirens.

Seconds later the rangers decided I was unqualified to drive code (lights and sirens) so I stopped in the road and switched out the cab for the jump seat in the back. Snapping the seat belt into position I started to feel the vehicle charge through traffic, and watched the scattered cars out of the rear window.

Up front there was radioing back and forth for the location. Still it it was unclear where the wreck was. We were heading out of the Valley on the one way road and it appeared we needed to cross the river to get onto Southside Drive.

The ambulance was beyond the east end constrictions and could open up fully with few cars holding us back. We arrived at El Cap cross-over, a short cut that allowed you to bridge the river and avoid driving the full length of the Valley to double back onto Southside Drive.

Sounded like taking this route would be the best thing. But there was a problem. A road surfacing project had just laid a fresh layer of asphalt and the road was blocked off.

No problem we had lights and sirens. Flashing and wailing the ambulance dodged traffic control, rounded a bollard and plunged into the gooey asphalt. I could hear us plowing the twin dark furrows as the sound of asphalt landing soggily on the bodywork entertained my ear drums.

I could see the road crew wading back in trying to repair the damage out the back window.

Slowly emerging from the asphalt the driver discovered that the road work further up the road meant that there was no way through after all. A three point turn and we headed back the way we had come in. Again the ambulance wallowed into the black asphalt soup. More plowing. Out the back window I could see the crew once again trying to repair the damage.

Back on the main road the ambulance opened up. This time the sirens were accompanied by the distinct pitter patter of asphalt flecks dropping off the chassis.

We made the turn onto Southside Drive. I could feel the seat belt tightening as we jostled through the Gauntlet, a series of bends from Pohono Bridge to Roosevelt Meadow. Now the ambulance could surge as the road straightened. Ding Dong Alley, the straight opposite Bridalveil Falls, was uncluttered by poor parking, tourists taking group photos while standing in the roadway or someone reorganizing their luggage by stacking it directly in traffic.

We were going to make it!

Arriving at the scene the front two piled out to respond. In the dark in the back I struggled to find the button to release the seat belt. It had got quite tight so my movement was restricted. I frantically ran my hands up, down and across looking for something to press. Very little light was available from the back windows so the main light sources were the small indicator bulbs that showed power levels for the various bits of medical equipment.

I was making no progress in finding the release button. I sat for a few minutes waiting for the driver to come back and release me. No one turned up.

I was going to have to find another way out. Relaxing

and pushing myself back into the seat I managed to get the seat belt to unlock. Slowly I worked slack into the system, pushing the chest strap away and trying to work the slack across the lap strap. I had to lock off the tension with one had before using the other hand to do the shuffle.

Finally I had enough room in the system to start to wriggle my body up and out of captivity. Eventually managing to get my hips up and out of the seat, get my feet under my butt and then stand and step out of the confines of the belt.

I took a moment to celebrate my escape before jumping out the door.

My colleagues were deep in conversation with the on scene ranger. I wandered up and asked what was happening. Max asked me where I had been. I told him I had been trapped in my seat. He smiled. He added he had only just noticed I was not around.

Where were the patients? We had taken so long to respond they had been rescued by another unit. Now it was time for us to head back to base. Which was a good thing as I was wearing shorts and the mosquitos were chewing me up.

Unfortunately one of us had to stay behind to work with tow truck crew. They pulled rank. I ended up hanging out in bug hell waiting for the winch crew. Hours later and with significant blood loss the car was extracted and I got back to the cache. Note to self, always wear pants on a call out.

~

SAR Team

Yosemite is something of an anomaly in the SAR world. Each season a couple of teams are recruited to live in the park and be available for call outs. The make up of the team has evolved from a rag tag band of Cobra willing dirt bags to a more professional group of dirt bags. They function as the primary response crew for carryouts, searches and recoveries. As a group they schedule their availability and burn their off hours on big wall ascents and vertical adventures. Living in the Valley, squeezed off to the edge of Camp Four they have an envied existence. As an AD (Administratively Determined) hire they get paid for each call out by the hour, with a sliding scale linked to the technical exposure of the mission and their role within it. AD hiring allows NPS to deal with sudden or unexpected emergency call outs. Most SAR units around the country do not have this option and rely solely on volunteers.

2

SEARCHING

Searching the river for a body relies mainly on luck. Typically you have a point last seen. That is a good place to start but much beyond that it is a bit of a crap shoot, apart from knowing you need to head downstream.

Working the river in high spring flow comes with its own set of challenges and dangers. Snowmelt varies with the weather and time of day. You have to gauge the right places to access and at what time. Sometimes the window does not exist to access the water and you are confined to the banks, high above the water scouring the rapids for a shot of color or hint of a body. Looking for birds scavenging is always a good clue.

Immediately after a call out specialist teams might probe the banks or immediate eddies below the point of entry. You always arrive on scene hoping to see a bedraggled figure hauled out on a midstream rock, alive and stable just waiting for rescue. It does not happen like that very often.

The calls can come in with vague references to locations.

People hike out to trailheads or finally get a cell signal and present a disjointed picture of where and what happened.

WHEN THE WATER is high in the spring the team finds time to swim rapids, play on the waves and get some swimming conditioning in. I loved these sessions, surfing waves and carving turns on the rescue boards.

On this afternoon the call out tone sounded to interrupt one of these sessions and I needed to shift from training to responding. Transitioning from fun to business, without removing my wetsuit, I jumped in a rig. Over the siren there was a discussion of options. The river was already high, and recent thunderstorms had flashed it higher. The first reports had indicated that the person had gone in near the Valley floor. I had river boarded the lower "closed" section many times during trainings and was familiar with the hazards. I had the confidence to run it as a solo hasty team for a quick scan if needed.

Arriving at the bridge the rig pulled to the curb and immediately a couple stepped forward. I grabbed the river board and fins as the ranger started interviewing the witnesses.

When did it happen?

Where did it happen?

Who went in and can they swim?

How big are they?

The incident had happened an hour before and they had hiked down to report it. A simple slip on the trail and their friend had pitched off the side and slid 50 feet down the granite into the river. There had been a fleeting glimpse of them as they hit the water and then they were gone.

We had to change plans.

I shifted my gear to walking mode, clipping my fins and rope to the back of the PFD. Details were radioed in as we jogged up the trail. You focus on maintaining a sustainable pace. Managing your energy for what you might have to do once you get on scene.

Eyes are kept down.Your haste and equipment begs questions from others on the trail. No eye contact means no opening for a conversation. The goal is to get on scene ASAP.

The point of entry was not clear. We missed it the first time and had to backtrack. Scanning the river all you could see was whitewater, few eddies and unsurvivable rapids with sharp toothed rocks staggering up out of the chaos.

Eventually we accessed the river's edge 300 feet below the point of entry and surveyed a small set of falls and the braided channel below. No signs. It was hard to see how someone would survive with the right gear let alone a backpack and hiking boots. The rain had stopped and sun was trying to warm things up.

Radio traffic confirmed no signs and the difficulty in safely operating in the immediate area. The sound of the helicopter rotors neared. It flew passes over the area using our physical location as a marker. The ship was so low the rotor wash chilled me in the wetsuit. They saw nothing and left to fly back to base.

The search moved to recovery. It was a slower trip back down the trail. No much talking between as we mentally prepared for what we would say to the friends.

By the time we made it down the trail we were too cold to engage with them on the bridge and it was left to others to give the bad news. Back in the car with the heater blasted I finally stopped shivering and started to discuss next steps.

It is impossible not to feel sadness when a mission does not have a positive outcome. You start with optimism and hope, maybe this time they will have enough luck to eddy out to safety. This quickly fades when the scene you arrive at presents nature at its most violent and unforgiving. There is an instantaneous switch in your mind from rescue to recovery. You might not articulate it but you know. Looking down at the river we knew there was not going to be a save. It was going to have sad outcome and it was going to take time to resolve.

Over the next few days spotters walked the trail and used binoculars to scope the rapids for a hidden answer. Nothing showed up for weeks until the report of some clothing being spotted in the area hung up midstream.

Dispatched to the scene to see if the items could be recovered the river has shifted character. Still running high and cold it had safer access. After scouting a swimmable line out to the island I geared up.

Before you hit the water there is plenty of double checking. My tether, quick release buckle and fins all eyeballed, tested and mentally noted. Zips pulled up and checked. PFD snugged, then lightly relaxed, I still need to be able to breath.

Making eye contact with my belayer I tapped my hand on top of my helmet signaling "am I ok to go?"

The belayer checked their stance and sent the same signal back to me "good to go". The belayer would swing me back to the shore if I blew the line and could not swim across. They were my backup.

Tourists hovered on the trail wondering what was happening. It is unavoidable in these high traffic zones.

Keep your eyes down and avoid opening the communication door.

I focussed on the swim. A short powerful tongue whipped along the left shore with a grabby eddy within 15 feet off to the right. With a high entry and some serious thrashing I could make the eddy before the rope drag proved too much and pulled me back into the current.

Visually checking with the belayer one more time I adjusted my feet stepping a little deeper and gauging the current's power.

Steady.

Steady.

Go.

The coldness hits first. Then the power. Intuitively I feel myself relax into the flow. No need to fight it, you need to work with it.

Beating a steady, un-panicked rhythm, I angled my body into the current and within four strokes popped up for a deep breath in the eddy. No time to slack as the safety rope was now exerting a pull of its own out in the current. Another stroke and a fishy flop on the bank anchored me. Taking a minute to get my breathing back I tapped my helmet again " I am ok"

My belayer responded with same signal " I see you are ok"

The fins came off and I slipped the safety rope to secure it to a root. Now on the island I could scramble to its foot and look for the clothing.

It was obvious, a bright flash of color wrapped around a rock. Although the water was deeper I could eddy hop behind a couple of big rocks to get next to the jacket. Reaching out it released without force. I crumpled it up and tucked it in my pfd to keep my hands free.

Back on the island the jacket got pulled out for investigation. Checking the language on the label it looked like it had come off our missing person. Hoping for more clues searching the far side of the island seemed like a good idea. It did not take long to survey the shallows, pick at the root balls and scan the rapids. Nothing was obvious. Now I was at the top of the island looking up at the Falls we had surveyed on the first day.

Suddenly a powerful smell hit my nose. Very strong. Decay.

Looking upstream nothing stood out.

The rock ledge that made up the mini falls was more exposed, the water no longer breaking across its entire length. Each chute was still full of foamy whitewater, rifling flow through narrow clefts. Standing in the flow would have been impossible but the midstream boulders now had eddies emerging behind them that offered limited shelter.

Another scan focussing in for a sign. Slower this time. Checking the shadows. Something catches my eye. Something on the eddy line cycled up. Waiting and watching. A piece of wood twists out of the current's grip. Just wood. Scanning again.

Seeing nothing it was time to get back across the current. This time it would be a pendulum move, no need to swim. With the belayer holding the rope tight I would swing across the current and under the far bank.

Grabbing the carabiner I reached behind and snapped into the D ring on the rescue vest. Habitually I slide the ring back and forth on the belt to check it was clipped into the right place.

All good.

Making eye contact across to the belayer I got the helmet tap.

"Ready to go"

"Ready to go"

I ran through the safety check one more time. Fins snapped on, pfd zipped, D-ring free to slide, shoulder straps snug, helmet clipped. And this time the recovered jacket was snug and buried against my chest.

Carefully I stepped into the current. Fins are awkward to walk in so they were angled downstream. The belayer pulled in the slack. One more glance across with a helmet bump.

As soon as the echoed sign was returned I launched. Making yourself long is the secret, arms across the chest and a gentle fin. The water pillows around the helmet, just relax and let the air pocket form. In a few moments I was bumping along the shore, sitting up in the shallows and signaling I was ok. The rope slackened and I could come out of the system.

Huddling together on the bank we checked out the jacket and compared notes. My belayer had not smelled or seen anything. We both surveyed from the shore. Nothing caught our eye.

Another day and no closer to finding the missing person?

A week later a patrol spotted the body hooked up at the surface right above one of the mini fall chutes. The water level was still too high to get to them from the water so it would have to be a high line.

Back on scene the team split to their tasks. A tree crew ascended to secure anchor points high up the trunk. A line was fired across the river and multiple ropes were hauled over to eventually form the high tensioned span that was needed. High above me the team played with angles to figure out how to get the line over the body.

Being down at the water's edge I would run safety in the event the line failed and the responder ended up the water.

Ropes were laid out to throw and locations were assessed for launch points for a baited swimmer rescue.

Upstream the body was visible, although you had to know where to look. It was draped across the top of a midstream boulder. The back was covered with a thin layer of algae and it looked like another rock. The legs were down deep, kept in place by the flow and the undercut.

The technician geared up with a full hazmat suit, body harness and PFD. They checked out the body position, looked at the river features and registered where I would be on the shore if things went sideways.

The high line crew confirmed all the knots were in the right place and the system components had been checked. The technician tied in and doubled checked the carabiners. A quick exchange of commands and their journey began. The start was easy as they were tracking down so it was just a matter of feeding rope out rather than hauling.

The technician radioed their progress calling for a stop when they felt they were directly above their target. Slowly they were lowered to perch barely in the water, with the body at their feet.

Bodies present in different ways. We were fortunate that this one had been in almost refrigerated conditions for weeks so was in one piece. The tech slung the hips with a special designed cinch that spread the load rather than cutting in. Some physical shifting confirmed the body would pop free before the operation shifted to hauling.

Arrangements had already been made to shut the neighboring trail when the hauling began. Rangers moved people back from photo vantage points and stopped foot traffic in the view shed. When everything was tight on the trial closures the hauling began. The technician was raised first before reaching down to guide the body up and out of the water. Once clear the retrieve crew began the physically demanding haul of 300 plus pounds. With no visitors on the trail the haul team had plenty of room to take advantage of, walking back the rope as a group without worrying about it blocking access.

Now high above the water the technician, all in white, and the sagging body, sadly bent double, moved across the backdrop of the cliffs and waterfalls. Looking up I could see the tech strong arming the cinch to avoid having to manage a spiraling body. They made steady progress to the shore where they paused.

A ground crew unzipped a heavy duty body bag and held it vertically. Radio traffic coordinated the body's lonely descent into the bank side shadows. Dropping the body directly into the bag made everyone's jobs easier. It was less intimate and less gooey than a hands on transfer. Unclipping the cinch from the carriage the body, in the bag, now rested on the ground.

The technician could now be lowered and the systems broken down. The trail was opened back up and steady hum of tourists could be heard above us.

The body bag was repositioned to let it drain more effectively. The smell was unmistakable. Death. A change in the drainage plan was needed. Confirming there were more bags available a couple of holes were cut at the foot and the draining continued.

Water is heavy and transport would be easier with less weight.

Above us the breakdown continued. Anchors were getting removed from the tree. Ropes were hauled back across the river and coiled. A hazmat bag appeared as the tech peeled off their layers and packaged them. Conversations were muted as we got our jobs done. I slipped out of my pfd, re-stuffed the throw ropes and stowed them away in my pack.

Ready to go.

The stokes litter arrived with the big wheel attached underneath. The wheel made the haul out so much easier. It cruised the rough trail, absorbing the bumps and drops leaving the attendants to concentrate on just balancing the load.

The body was sheathed in a second bag and lifted into the litter. Seat belts snapped across it holding it in place. A rope was attached to the uphill end and trailed out to technician, who would hold it as an additional braking option.

Sets of hands grabbed the rails and listened in for a command to move. Experience had taught us to move quick on the trail. Shouts ahead cleared the way and we kept our eyes down.

Off the litter went. The trail was full again but the crowds scattered as the procession rolled by. It was happening so fast I am unsure if people registered that there was a body racing by them. The brake rope kept us from losing control but it was still felt like a sprint.

At the bridge junction the team dove left and grabbed the horse trail. There would be less foot traffic and vehicles could get to a closer point for pick up.

Everyone was sweating now, but it was nearly over. A couple of tighter turns told us the uphill portion was coming. Unspoken, grips were adjusted and shoulders shrugged pack straps.

As soon as the flat was hit the pace picked up, now the team was running. Accelerating up the little rise, maintaining the momentum and not letting the dead weight hold us back. Breathing hard now. A few more yards and out of the trees into the parking lot.

A moment to catch our breath while the wheel was popped off. Now you could feel the weight. Two hands on the rail, knees bent.

So heavy.

The team pivots to shuffle the litter, first to balance on the tailgate and then slide into the flat bed. The tail gate snaps shut.

The cargo is invisible to all but those peeping over the edge.

When it rolls by the bus stop no one will think deeper thoughts spurred by the image. They won't see anything to distract them from their thoughts of pizza or beer.

The death remains hidden.

As do its lessons.

3

RECOVERY

After three days on the river training I was happy to be cracking a beer and eating fatty snacks. The early season flow was high and cold. Training means you spend a lot of time in the water doing rotations.

It saps you. Arms get heavier. Movement gets sluggish. At the end of the session removing your wetsuit almost proves too much.

In the background the call out tone rang out on the radio. There had been a jumble of radio traffic just before it but not much attention was lent while I had a bottle in one hand and a sandwich in the other.

It was a Swiftwater callout. Numerous witnesses had reported a visitor had fallen in the creek and the responding ranger could see a body pinned a short way off shore.

Putting down the beer and taking a final bite of sandwich we grabbed a pile of wet gear and jumped into a rig. Lights and sirens. More radio traffic, a confirmation of the location and site description.

Arriving on scene there was a long line of emergency vehicles. We geared up and hustled up to the incident commander. The light was beginning to dim but you could make out the submerged body, head face down, arms outstretched. They had been in the water long enough for this to be a recovery.

Shore based efforts were underway. They ranged from a large blunt hook on an extension pole to weighted ropes. All of them were being utilized to try to snag the body . Hopefully it be could popped out and recovered downstream.

Seemed like a reasonable plan. The adjacent trail was one of most heavily foot trafficked in the Valley. So getting the incident tied up without dealing with a full spectator gallery the next day was desirable.

Todd and I teamed up and were assigned to be on the other side of the river as a baited swimmer set up. Baited swimming involves one responder being attached, via a quick release belt, to a rope while a shore based belayer helped to keep them safe on a taunt line. Modern pfd's incorporate these systems into their design, but it needs good training and a continual awareness to be safe. They weren't called draining vests for nothing.

The IC wanted us in position quickly. They wanted to pop the body before it got dark so every minute counted. Below the victim's pin point the river braided out into narrow channels with frequent strainers and unstable rocky banks.

We forded the first channel with no issue. Todd carried a couple of extra throw bags and I had an awkwardly packed bag of anchor material. In the water it acted as an anchor.

In front of us the main channel held most of the flow. Off the steep right bank there was short section without woody debris spanning the width. Not an ideal crossing point but it was what we had.

Todd geared up to swim with the rope attached to his

baited swimmer belt. It took some time to find the launch point but finally he had a stance. With high flows Todd decided to shallow dive as far out into the current as possible. He hoped there would be enough momentum with a couple of big strokes and kicks to grab the powerful eddy pumping along the left shore. My job was to manage the rope going out so there was enough to allow Todd to get across but not so much that there was downstream drag to pull him back out into the current.

He got a perfect launch. He pancaked into the water, angled almost upstream, and with whirling limbs powerfully grabbed the eddy before he stuck his head up breathing hard.

Now it was my turn. I would be pendulumed across on a loaded rope. With my unruly luggage all I had to do was relax, face down stream and let the physics do the work. I attached the rope to the ring behind me, double checking it was free to slide, and crouched in the water with a hand on shore. That beer had made itself through my body and I felt a desperate nervous need to pee.

Exchanging signals with Todd I knew he was ready. He had sat down at the head of the eddy perfectly positioned to anchor, then allow me to swing across the current. Humping the luggage up on my chest, then sitting back into the current I pushed off the bank. The luggage was unbalancing, pitching my head momentarily under water. Allowing the luggage to shift off to the downstream side, my body floated up and I could breath again.

I got the eddy easily and disconnected from the belay. Todd was already looking upstream and could see a stance that might work. He was visualizing the next steps. I took the time to have that pee.

Hugging the shore and then working across a shoal we

set up a little below the body. With water flowing around us the only way to stabilize was sit down in the water and dig my heels in. Freezing water below the waist was quickly uncomfortable.

Todd clipped in again and confirmed the plan. If the body cut loose he would launch and land on it. I would simply hang on, trying to swing the combined weight of the body and Todd into the shallows.

Saying it out loud made it sound less than a good idea. Both of us checked in again. Todd decided that he would only jump if he could easily grab it, he wasn't going to swim for it. And it had to be close.

This sounded like a much better idea.

No radios so we signaled upstream that we were ready. Todd turned and checked in that I had him. Eyeing the debris downstream I assured him I did.

The extraction efforts began. The pole and ropes were vigorously pulled from different directions. An arm would break the surface. The shoulders would appear but the head would always stay under. The body was not shifting. And light was almost gone.

Sitting shivering in the shallows with Todd braced to launch at any second we were both tiring fast. It was relief to be waved off from our station. Repacking the gear we eyed the exit route. A short stumbling swim through a deep channel and the left shore was gained. A shuffle stepped jog down the horse trail and we popped out on a bridge for pickup.

The next morning the extraction efforts resumed. The team was bigger and more rigging was underway when I pulled up. A ladder had been rigged off the right bank. It extended out over the water with ropes spidering out from above to the sides to stabilize and support it. Eddie had managed to snag a couple of slings around the body to provide a reliable point to attach the haul systems.

Our team set up a little further upstream on the opposite side. A pile of mid stream boulders provide plenty of monumental anchor points to thread. The haul systems exerted multiplied forces that could displace what appeared to be solid placements. Everything was checked and rechecked. And monitored.

The body was on the surface now. Pinned by an ankle it pointed downstream and rippled along with the water. Overnight the river had worked the clothing loose and washed it away. It was naked in the flow.

The rope crews had started to tension the systems. One set pulled the body vertically while the others worked to move it back upstream, against the flow. Over the radio directions called for more, or less tension, as they watched for signs of the body coming loose.

The operation was trying to conclude before the first pulse of visitors walked by. Operations had used a bus to reduce the most immediate view point and stationed enough uniforms to keep people moving along. But it was going to be better for everyone is we could get the body out of the river before the day hikers really got going.

Breakfast was delivered while we waited for something to happen. Greasy breakfast muffins with egg and bacon were perfect fuel for the assignment. I felt pretty removed from the reality of what we were doing as I munched on my second one, perched on a boulder 15 feet from the body.

The haul systems appeared to be making little progress. I wondered out loud what would happen if the body simply came apart? If the forces were so great how would we deal with that scenario?

It was at that moment the body came free and shot in

the air. It cartwheeled above the water, the load lines seesawing and bouncing as the opposing forces found a new balance point. I registered it had one sock on.

Shouted instructions now. The body was going to come our way. Somehow slack came in the system and the body was back in the water. It began to swing my way in the current.

Things were happening very fast. Our team was scrambling along the bank and I got a shouted instruction to grab the body. I was unsure what to do so I hauled on the nearest rope. The body bumped across the shallows and eddied out below me.

I just froze and stared. It was the first time I had been on this type of recovery, this close to body. I had seen bodies before but not like this. The others piled in the water to secure it with their hands.

Brett registered I was struggling to comprehend what I was looking at. My assignment shifted to downstream safety as the ropes were released and body bag appeared.

Still I could not look away though. The eyes were shut but the mouth gaped open. Lifeless without rigor they flopped about, sagging and un-compliant in their death. And naked. Apart from the sock.

I have no idea how long it took to heave them into the bag. Nor do I have any recollection of what happened next. Where we carried the bag? No closing memories because the entire episode stops with the body coming out the water and swinging ashore.

I pass the spot often. I have used it for teaching, walking through the entry point to the pinning location and played out the recovery. One summer, in low water, I swam and splashed my way through the route they must have taken.

Where they fell in is next to a fiercely undercut boulder

followed by a sharp edgy chute. They might have taken a head shot early on and not known much about what was about to happen. That's what you hope. The chute squeezes between two big boulders and spits out into the wider channel where they pinned.

It is harder to pick out that location. Seasonal flows changes the river bed and I can only estimate where it might have been. The water would not have been deep, three or four feet, but it was flowing very fast when they became entrapped.

I recognize where I had stood and looking downstream where Todd set up the night before. The ladder rigging spot on river right is obvious.

Climbing out I watch the visitors stream by on foot and bike. They are laughing and enjoying their day out. People stop for photos and memory moments. They are happily oblivious to the tragedy of the spot. On a hot summer day there is no relating to a spring slip off the shore.

Like so many places here that have this dark thread of tragedy hidden in plain view.

4

WAKING UP DEAD

I first heard the phrase responding to the guest's death at one of the lodges. Looking for more information in preparation for talking with the family I had asked the usual questions around the timeline and events. By all accounts the visitor had had a great hike the previous day. They had talked to the front desk about potential other trails, had a nice meal at the restaurant and retired, according to their group, around 10pm. When they did not appear for breakfast, failed to respond to phone calls and hammering on their door the front desk had let themselves in.

The guest appeared asleep. A quick check for a pulse confirmed that they had passed away. The rangers had responded and chatted with the group. I was over to start the process of reaching out to family members and sort out next steps.

There was nothing to indicate what had caused their death, they had woken up dead.

Calling the deceased's sibling we talked through what was known, how they had been found and what the plan was. The conversation turned to reflection on their sibling's life. How much they loved the park. When they had first visited. Which trail was their favorite.

There were questions directed about me. How I had come to the park? Why I stayed? The sibling listened and reflected on my answers and what was similar to their families experience.

Inevitably the idea emerged that there was some peaceful satisfaction for the family that their relative had died in a place that they loved. Tucked up in bed after a busy day. They had spent the evening laughing and telling stories with friends, planning for a next day that never happened.

The family suggested just bagging them up and hiding the body under a big boulder. They felt that the sibling would have enjoyed that. Hidden forever in the place they loved the most. Recognizing that it was not an option they determined the best location to scatter their ashes. Access was discussed. Which trails were open when. When would the snow melt out and the roads open.

Details.

All calm. There were jokes about the sibling's love of a good glass of wine and chocolate. Tales of where they had explored and what they had planned for next summer.

Back to details.

Discovering I was English there was a complete derailing of the conversation into my thoughts on the monarchy (an expensive anachronism) and what my football team was? (Aston Villa).

Details.

Exchanging the funeral home's number I asked if there anything more they needed from me. There was a pause. A mumbled thank you. One more question. They wanted to be absolutely sure that the eyes had been shut when the body was discovered.

Yes. They appeared asleep.

Silence.

You let it sit, give people time to formulate, unhurried, their thoughts. It is all part of being present, not filling space verbally. Avoiding uninvited input. Just sharing the quiet.

"Thank you again, they really loved Yosemite. So many happy memories. If it had to happen somewhere, the Valley felt right."

5

REVIEW

Lessons happen every mission. Things that work get refined through practice. Teams chat through pros and cons in their response. Changes happen through failures. Big failures lead to program suspension while protocols are examined and rewritten.

Reviews during a busy season can be on the fly. A hasty gathering during the demob (demobilization) with the team leaders talking through the incident play by play. Individuals pipe in their experience and responsibilities. Points are raised for consideration and future implementation. Afterwards it is back to the gear and prepping for the next call out.

Operations are easy to deconstruct and dissect. It is about systems and how they are deployed then utilized. They work or don't work. How resources are dispatched to a specific location, their timing and scale becomes a mathematical problem.

The human element is the challenging element to review. The team is made up of a spectrum of characters and personalities who all process experiences in different ways.

My early experiences with debriefing the human element was a guarded group activity that few really engaged with. Some for good reason as their professional lives were at stake if they made an honest declaration of where they were at. Sitting circled up days after the mission you would be led through a replay of the sounds, sights and sensations you may have experienced. Then magically an hour later, after some interchanges, the facilitators would leave with the supposed healing complete.

It did not work like that. Conversations would happen on the side with carefully screened friends to ensure the opinions expressed went no further. Or dark humor, fueled by alcohol, would allow the traumatic images to get vomited out for review. Addled brains would dimly process the events, storing memories away in a recess to dysfunctionally guide daily life and rot relationships.

There is a clock ticking inside every responder that records every second of traumatic exposure and banks it for a future breakdown. People discount it and say not me. And for some on the surface it appears true. But examine the road they are on and patterns emerge. Unhealthy choices, bingeing, bickering. Insignificant disagreements fester up in metastasized misdirected rage.

There is a reckoning at some point. Alone or publicly the dam breaks and the toxicity pours out. Returning from a deployment I watched a colleague morph from a life time of caustic high performance into an emotional sponge of good-will. They had been transformed by their exposure to a humanitarian disaster, it had been the trigger to void the lifetime of disturbing memories. Others have walked away from SAR when scooping up the last body recovery proved too much.

There is an accumulated sadness that comes with

working close to trauma. Your processing ranks can close to only those that have the same experience and that narrowed focus chokes perspective. You exist in the echo chamber, the emotions trapped in exclusive companionship.

Some do find the way out. They find their healthy practice that lets them breath air into their bodies and dispel the memory mist. They flush their body with endorphins through physical activity or doing the happiest thing they know. By feeling the soil beneath their toes, the smooth embrace of granite or the cold immersive slap of cold water on their face they reset.

After a big mission I set aside a full day for disfunction. Having goals is a bit pointless on these days apart from getting outside to pump my legs and get my lungs screaming. Which as an asthmatic is fortunately pretty easy. If I can get some naps, chat with family and friends about good stuff, and eat, recovery begins to happen.

Mentally it is a more targeted exercise with deeper conversations with peer counsellors who go beyond the "how are you doing and what are you feeling" classics. There is a download aspect to these chats. A shedding of the weighty mix of administrative reporting and emotional reaction.

After a summer of being on point for too many deaths as a Family Liaison Officer I broke. Tears flowed without warning and I sought out solitude to deal ineffectively with the burden. Fortunately the warmth of friends rescued me. Shared dinners, quiet walks, borrowed dogs and laughter all drew me back.

Still slivers of memories hover. There is fading, but a remnant is hooked in my brain that will never be flushed. A psyche scar. Hidden but there.

It was a relief to be introduced to the Stress Continuum.

Originally developed as a tool by the Marine Corps to assess combat readiness in troops it has morphed into a practical tool for dealing with stress and emotional traumatic injury.

Sitting in the classroom on the first day and hearing the explanations around ready, reacting, injured and critical categories I felt elated by its disclosure. Suddenly the jagged journey my brain had been on made sense. And the way back began to be charted.

The stress continuum baselines when someone is ready. Performing is another word for it. Color coding this state as existing in green. It details healthy relationships with people, and substances. Emotional, physical health and routines. Calling out a sense of purpose...vitality.

As an individual transitions through reacting (yellow) to injured (orange) and finally critically injured (red) each category deteriorates. A mapped descent from function.

When the instructor described the inability to deal with complexity as a key diagnostic in being critically injured all my alarms started going off. This all sounded very familiar.

Confronted with all but the simplest binary decisions my brain would freeze up. Opening a fridge to make a sandwich would overload my capacity to decide what I wanted. Colors, textures, jars, Tupperware, sell by dates. All too much.

An inability to deal with complexity. I chose hunger. Nutrition was too complex.

But now I recognized what was happening and why. The physiological impacts on my body, my sleep patterns, everything was affected by this residual sorrow. And slipping into this state had happened while life had been so good.

Flipping to green and starting to scribble notes it was easy to remember what it had been like to be in that state and how it could be sustained. Contact with friends. Doing the things that brought joy. Being in or on the water. Physically active each day. Putting the computer away and escaping the blue light. Reading something apart from current affairs. Celebrating life. Do the things I used to do.

Now my boat sits on the roof rack every day ready for the river. On the commute when I feel the pull to get home early, instead of unloading and stumbling over the rounded rocks to the water, I listen to the river. Its chatter over the shallows with the eddy line churn sings the song that in a split second resets my body and brain.

Finding the balance point as I settle into the cockpit, flexing the paddle into the current's pull the world floats away.

Solely transfixed on the bow wave ripple the weight on my shoulders lifts as the muscles flow and stress drains.

Savoring the arcing drops of water off the blade on the recovery stroke I strive for the perfect forward stroke.

Millions of strokes in I have not found it yet but what I have discovered saves me.

For more information on the Stress Continuum check out the Responder Alliance and the work of Laura McGladerray.

6

FIRE

Until you are right next to a fire it is hard to appreciate the overwhelming power it possesses. Out on the veldt in Southern Africa we drove through a fast moving grass fire racing it to the valley rim before our descent home.

Crossing the fire front the cindered smoke choked out the sense of direction. Speed dropped. The heat penetrated the cab, along with the greedy snap crackle of the flames. The car inched forward feeling the road's direction through the gravel crunch of the tires as the smoke arrowed by.

Slowly a grey light wedge appeared and allowed more speed. Bursting through the engine adjusted to clearer air we pulled clear. My palm hovered over the window feeling the heat. Reaching the drive way we dropped below the smoke, free wheeling to the ranch on an empty tank. Stalled from climbing the final bump to the house I stepped out and looked over my shoulder. The evening breeze had kicked up slope, stalling the flames as the sun set into the haze slowly leaking a solar seam across the valley crest. As night fell the fire starved of fuel slipped into the darkened surrender.

In Australia uncomfortably close to a bush fire I remember seeing, feeling and hearing the fire flash across a road and explode with a thrilling roar. Minutes later driving out ahead of the fire front, adrift in smoke, the windscreen filled up with brumby hides as the wild horses too sought escape. It felt like a thrilling game rather than survival.

Decades later our fire world has changed. The ignitions are more frequent, their intensity greater and everyone seems to know someone who has lost a home or had a narrow escape. Smelling smoke in the air an informal phone tree kicks in to try and establish where it might be coming from.

Has someone called it in?

Scanning local feeds and listening in on radio traffic you can figure out locations and scale. New applications mean I can watch how air attack had been dispatched with real time data confirming the direction and speed of the air tanker even as I watch it fly over my house.

Marking the fire's location I look for wind patterns to figure out where the smoke is going and if the fire is heading our way. If it is close possessions get shifted to the car, they have been sitting in a box ready for this all summer. The decisions about what will be left behind was made long ago. Another check of the feed. Initial attack has started to knock it down, but they are keeping an eye on it. Boxes come out of the car and sat back in the corner.

You function in this space for months.

You and your community.

Always vigilant, ready to move and respond. Reducing fuel means raking up the pin needles, burning them at tail end of the winter. Chopping trees down that overhang the roof and clearing a defendable space around your physical structures. You are manicuring your wild space to harden it against fire.

Neighbors hold rigid to their favorite tree accommodated by a hole in their deck. Never mind its spread boughs could fail with a winter loading of snow or cascade an ember torrent onto their roof.

Transplants bring a myopic ignorance to the neighborhood naively embracing their sense of wild and denying their responsibilities to protect it. Responsible property owners manage their property to not only guard the structure but to protect firefighters lives. Irresponsible property owners lazily rely on others to protect them and preach against fuel reduction in angsty columns to local newspapers.

WHEN I HEARD about the latest ignition I was not too worried. There was plenty of territory between it and us. Steep and densely timbered it had plenty of fuel to burn and it was sparsely inhabited to the south. Going east it would start hitting property and communities quickly, but there was an evacuation route. Heading north it would run into previously burned areas reasonably quickly, potentially stalling it's spread and reducing its intensity.

Over the next couple of days it grew significantly. The threat to the east required communities to begin evacuation and the small gateway town of El Portal became ghostly quiet, quick.

With the operation area bisected by the Merced River Incident Command approached SAR for support with river crossings. So I found myself inadequately dressed again in flip flops and shorts patrolling the river bank assessing access points and staging areas. The assessment turned into a 14 day assignment to coordinate the teams ferrying fire fighters and supplies across the river.

My commute took me through the road block above the canyon with a leisurely drive along the river. I would pass staged crews and gear. Getting closer to the active fire zone nerves would start up. Debris would be in the road. Fallen smoking logs. Blackened rocks lay shattered in the lane. Heavy smoke settled in a choking silence. Occasional flashing lights strobed out of the swirl. Sometimes I could follow a plow, it felt safer as the giant blade bullied the road clear.

Each day I could map the fire's progress up the canyon. It was edging up the flanks and only the inversion layer that set up each night seemed to be stalling it out. This weather pattern was buying the firefighters time to build defensible space around buildings and communities in its path. Ahead of the fire bulldozers constructed fire breaks, crews chopped, then raked, clear bare earthed paths before laying snaking hose-line up impossible slopes.

River operations was split with a team mid canyon and my team in El Portal. Arriving at the staging area I could get a briefing of what was happening over the day. Gear was pulled from the trailer and set up for ferrying crews. Rafts topped off after a chilly night in the water. Work-wise it was a narrow window of activity. A morning ferry of a crew to continue prepping the hand line up the old incline to Camp One. Occasional ferries during the day for command staff. An evening sunset pick up of the tired but burly crew at the end of their shift.

During the day I would amble up to the roadway and eyeball the latest smoke conditions. Afternoon wind patterns changed with smoke clearing out and flames starting to shoot skyward. By the evening commute the air was full of sparks and you would feel the heat of the flames driving home through the active zone.

Sky cranes hoovered water up out of the river, hovering their blades at road level with leaves scattering in their wash. Pilots threaded the narrowest ports to grab more water and return to hotspot drops. Crews assembled on the roads, fire blackened and dog tired. The fires created lightning jagged etches up the slopes with spiraling flames. Driving out early evening I watched the fire consume an old historic hotel on the north side of the river and sensed the gold mine camp at Ned's Gulch would follow suit in a few hours. Fully engaged the building stood stark shadowed within the fireball that consumed it.

A day later, snugged in behind a convoy of fire engines, I watched embers cascade off a roadside cliff and pepper my hood. The next day I switched from my casual beach wear to a full Nomex outfit with boots.

The fire was crawling with a determined ashy hand eastwards.

By day 11 it was at our doorstep. Helicopters began dropping fire starters on the ridge top as others ferried bright flashed retardant to fortify the hand line up Henness Ridge. Trees flamed up as bright candled flares against the night. Logs began rolling downslope, in turn lighting brush. Command was trying to deny the fire fuel and black-line it into submission. (A black line can be a deliberately lit area that burns fuels under controlled conditions to create a fire break).

The following morning the fire had stalled in places, but had reenergized, then jumped the line and was currently gobbling up the north facing slope of beetle killed pines and a century's worth of fire suppression. We inserted a monitoring crew ahead of the flames to check out an archeology site and then quickly had to extract them as the fire accelerated along the bank. Discussions about staging areas changed and our team was readied to evacuate to a safer zone if the fire decided to jump the river. There was a seriousness to conversations, less small talk looking at a distant smoke plume now you could feel the fire heat on your face. Rafts were transferred to trailers ready for redeployment up stream. Vehicles flipped to point in the direction of evacuation. From our staging point I could see flames racing up the north side flaring manzanita yards from the gas station. Evacuation routes changed.

Hundreds of fire fighters, vehicles and helicopters had shaped the fires path but not denied it passage. Miles of hose deployed over the last week now lay charged ready for the fire's chimneyed energy as it made the turn to race up the Indian Creek drainage. My shift was ending on the Ferguson Fire but it was leaving well charred memories of the practical courage of those who choose to battle fire on the ground and from the air. And the impossible task they face, and ultimate price that some pay, responding to a century of misguided fire suppression, poorly thought out development and selfish behavior.

THE FERGUSON FIRE *burned nearly 97,000 acres over a month in 2018. Two firefighters lost their lives during operations.*

7

ICE

The inner dialogue always hopes it is not me that makes the discovery. I am never sure what the reaction will be walking up on an accident scene. Sometimes the bile kicks up in my mouth at the scene of the bloody carnage. On other scenes I have shifted into a disassociated state, completing tasks without second thoughts and operating without immediate emotion. Personally it depends on who's in charge at the scene and how they project themselves into the space where stuff needs to get done. Calm, clear leadership leads to focussed performance.

With ice on the rocks and a high freeze in the mountains the river level had dropped precipitously. The team could now access the more technical terrain of the gorge and search the boulder gardens that high flows had denied them.

The river bed had been split between two teams, each team made up of two swift-water technicians. Shouted coordination between the teams ensured that each nook and cranny got visually checked out as they zigged, then zagged their way up the river bed.

The opening reach searched was low angle and wide. The water teams waded knee deep through still pools and peered, flashlight in hand into the darker recesses. The foot teams patrolled the higher bank relaying hints of up coming terrain and suggesting access points.

The first deep pool was encountered within an hour. The banks had steepened, with the foot teams ledging out and having to backtrack to a new vantage point. The deeper water required me to sink below the surface, the icy cold water shocking the head and leaving me gasping for breath. Adjusting the dry suit to vent out the excess air the cold began to seep into my limbs. The suit compressed around my body as a chilly wrap. Maybe I should have added more insulating layers?

After traversing the pool the searching challenge changed. Giant boulders and scattered log jams all needed to be probed and eyeballed for clothing or remains. Any color distracted the eye. A bottle top, energy bar wrapper or sock all offered a break up to the natural world palette. They flagged something worthy of investigation but none, as it turned out were of importance.

The water teams had leapfrogged each other and our assignment was a large pool below the first real cascade of the day. Perched above the pool we debated how to access it. The surrounding rocks presented a high, intimidating edge that offered a poor view of the pool immediately below. Unable to gauge the pool's depth the idea of taking a running jump off the edge was discarded. Ultimately we figured out a way to suspend one of us off the edge in a secure enough position that the other could climb down them then drop a shorter, safer distance into the water. My search partner was built like an armored vehicle so it was pretty obvious the lanky English guy was going to be the one shimmying down the human rope into the water.

Once he was wedged in position I started the downward climb. This happened much quicker than either of us anticipated. Given that the human rope had just got out of the water they were still pretty slippery and so I slid, rather than climbed down to their feet. Reaching their feet I had gained enough velocity to simply fly by them and plunge into the water.

There was a big splash without hitting the bottom. Having forgotten to vent my suit, again, it had been a rapid deceleration when the over inflated suit ballooned on impact, leaving me bobbing with wildly swollen shoulders and arms. I called up the drop would be fine and vented my suit.

Cold again.

With both of us floating in the water we began to laugh. Solely focussed on accessing the area we had not considered how to get out. The upper cascade was more ice than water and the exit looked like it was going to be a technical climb up a moderate face with inadequate footwear. Flexible dive boots do not offer great traction or toe pointing on vertical ice.

My partner truck off across the pool to check out the options and I proceeded to search. The deeper water was clear enough to feel confident nothing was hiding in the depths. The banks were easy to check out and all that remained was an entry slot where the water coursed through from upstream.

My team mate was already out of the water. He was chatting with the other team as he stood on the overflow's icy edge, deciding which side of the river to search next.

I had one area left to search in the pool. A smooth sided granite slot cut back from the flow. It held a flotsam raft of woody debris and plastic bottles. Bodies can bump up under these rafts requiring searchers to nose through them, gently pushing the debris curtain aside to check out the shadows below. The only way to access the slot was to dive below a guard rock roof and pop back up into the debris raft.

I held position in the deeper water, preparing for the temperature shock with deep breaths and getting my head together. I had already visually checked out things below the surface but no light penetrated the mass so I would have to go in and move things around.

I became focussed on what the feeling would be like if, popping up in the space, my immediate companion were a decomposing body. Physically shaking my head I tried to dislodge the thought. Water drops scattered off the helmet and rained on the surface. My hands reached up, steadying against the granite for the quick duck dive.

One more breath. Steady. The visual of a bobbing body popped up into my mind.

Maybe one more breath. Shaking the thought out again. More raindrops.

Now go.

It was a moment underwater before I was neck deep in the raft. Wood bumped up against my face, no body yet. In the rush of ducking in my eyes had closed so I still needed to drop down to check out below. My arms swept below the raft patrolling for a submerged mass. Nothing bumped against my hands.

Carefully brushing wood to the side a narrow slot opened up and light started to filter down. A quick dip under confirmed no body was hidden in the space. Huge relief.

The soundscape had changed as I emerged back into the flow. The other team was racing across the lip above, they had found something.

I kicked up to the cascade's foot. Ice was everywhere. My partner had executed an impressive ascent along the left shore somehow ascending a steep icy pitch with inadequate equipment and supreme confidence. I lacked the confidence but shared the equipment. I needed to find an alternate route.

Looking to the side the cascade was made up of three rounded ledges. All were coated with ice. By utilizing an entire body smear I could find enough traction to make upward progress. All be it slow progress.

Like a confused seal I inched my way to the top. It was so cold my outfit froze to the ice and provided a tenuous Velcro stability to my journey.

By the time I topped out, all the teams had swarmed the area. A body had been discovered and now everyone was focussed in on the extraction.

I moved in to position to help. The body was unhooked from the rock sieve and washed down into the body bag. Trying to keep the bag open I dropped my flashlight and it backlight the recovery with its underwater LCD beam.

Bumping through the shore side boulders the team worked the bag to the river's edge. Drained of excess water the remains were light and easy to move.

More coordination was needed before the traverse across the last pool. Leadership shouted back and forth confirming the route and what needed to happen. The shore team stationed up the steep bank to pass the bag, hand over hand, up to the trail.

A final check with the water team. All hands on the bag. The remains were floated across the pool.

Hands on, never alone.

I sat on the shore as the team relayed their cargo to the brim.

Gear was stowed, pockets zipped and doubled checked. Fins and ropes clipped to hiking mode. Tighten my shoes. My helmet was clipped to my shoulder strap. Scan for forgotten items.

A last look at the recovery site. Nothing special to draw your attention to it. A hidden history for a family now.

Time to get up into the sun and bring them home.

8

AIR

G lacier Point is 3000 feet above the Valley floor. From the viewing area with a rock wall, plus a railing, between you and the drop it feels safe to lean out to ponder the distance from top to bottom.

I can see plenty from this vantage point. Tiny dots scaling Snake Dike to summit Half Dome. The relic oxbows hinting at the Merced River's wandering odyssey before people constrained it with bridges, roads and infill. Knowing where to look I can pick out the splintering track of the rock fall that hit Curry Village in 2008.

The rocky talus, granite fingered, edges out from the margins. Buildings butt up against, and into, this active zone. Any construction optimism is short lived with abandonment on the cards for those that ignore the boulder strewn history around them.

Geologically the Valley is always moving material from top to bottom, trying to fill the ditch. There is a thin Valley strip that appears out of the flood and rock fall zone, but that remains open to question.

Rocks do not choose when to fall. An eon of balanced

time, the heat of a summer day, an expanding icy wedge or just too much rain all trigger failure.

Standing in Awahnee Meadow I had watched the third rock fall that tickled the hotel and forced its evacuation. The slow tipping yawl of the block then shattering percussive impact. Responding to the Curry Village rockfall I wandered through the airborne granite flour that dusted response and hung a hazed blanket across the Valley floor.

There is no planning prior to a rock's plummet.

Base jumpers do plan their plummets.

With my back against the railing I watched the base jumper step out of the manzanita. My first thought was that they were putting a lot of trust in a flimsy track suit and tiny backpack. They posed for a moment, arms out stretched and legs spread wide.

A flight check?

Groups of tourists barely gave them a glance. The distraction of the Alpenglow on the High Sierra more alluring than a track-suited figure on the cliff edge.

Moments later they cartwheeled off the edge and whooshed into the gathering shadows. Their drop had a sound, but in the darkness there was no visual clue to their progress. Up top their departure had generated no collective breath catch, or rush, to the railing. I waited for a canopy bloom but the inkiness gave nothing up.

If it was not seen had it happened?

Unwitnessed, just the way base jumpers seemed to like it.

THE BLACKHAWK FLIGHT came directly overhead. Everyone stopped and stared skywards. We tracked it out of sight and then returned to the task of hauling the body out of the river. Hung up on the left shore it had been easy to unpin and until the interruption of the President's flight had been going smoothly. I wondered if we had been seen from one of the ports. Maybe we should get the packaging done quickly?

HELICOPTERS ARE a vital part of the SAR response system. They insert teams into remote locations. Long line equipment for missions. Conduct intricate grid searches for clues about the disappeared, lost or missing. Respond with precision to a hotspot with a bucket of water or a mid-cliff pick off.

The crew respond to the most challenging situations. Missions that have a clock ticking to get medical aid on the ground ASAP. They witness the battle to save life yet too often end up transporting bodies that no amount of speed would have changed the outcome.

Waiting at the Landing Zone means staying out of the way. The HeliTac crew is a high functioning team that knows its job and calls the shots. They guarded a perimeter that crept in as the litter approached the meadow. Dangling below the helicopter's belly it rotated through the descent.

The ground crew slowly moved in as the litter touched down. The long line was released and the litter was smoothly lifted as the team began the transfer. Leaning over the Suburban back seat I reached to grab the bag as the bodies were shipped on board. They felt light as I rolled them into position.

The ground crew stepped back as the vehicle exited the meadow. A slow reset to focus on the living. The next task at hand.

Above the helicopter moved onto its next task. It is a machine with four beating hearts.

THE FIRE WAS RACING up the north side. Steep ground and lots of manzanita will do that. Sitting on a crash barrier on the opposite side of the canyon I was on the phone to my boss reporting out what I was seeing. We needed to evacuate staff from housing ahead of the fire and I was giving an update on the fire's progress up towards Foresta.

Air support had arrived quickly and the tankers had begun to drop loads. Instantly their presence made a difference knocking flames down, so much so that I walked back from the watching crowd to call in that things were looking good and the threat was lifted.

From the barrier there was a collective cry.

One person shouted "No" and just started running up the road. Turning with the phone to my ear I could see a cascading fireball rolling down the cliff.

From the railing people started talking loudly.

Statements. Observations. Questions.

It just augured in.

Something came off.

Is that survivable?

Lots of soundbites, no answers.

The flames fell out of sight. Dark smoke billowed up.

"The plane just crashed......." I cannot remember what I said, but I babbled on the phone before getting off. People were up off the rail and wandering, talking with distraction as they replayed what they had just seen.

Cameras were being reviewed and witnesses kept

repeating their version. Processing in real time. The fire raged as a backdrop to a collective shocked energy.

The entertainment thrill of the swoop and dump of the air show had disappeared. Now it was the discomfort of being a reluctant witness to a disaster. Not knowing what to do or say the crowd broke up. Cars pulled carefully out as muted pedestrians headed home.

Wandering back to the railing I was on the phone again babbling and raging. My boss suggested I go home. Looking across the canyon there were different smoke flavors belching skywards, the fuel tinged black smoke telling a story that happened in a moment and ended a lifetime.

9

LUCK

The couple had not made it to their hotel and family members had not heard from them for a few days. They had been due to drive up and over to the East Side on the Tioga Road, a beautiful Alpine drive that bisects the park. There are plenty of pull offs and viewpoints along the way.

Forests taper off as the road ascends and rolls around granite domes, skirts lakes and meadows before plummeting down to Lee Vining. It has steep drop offs on the sides and taking your eye off the road ahead for a moment can be problematic.

The helicopter had made numerous passes along the route with spotters looking for flashes of color in the trees.

Ground teams has been assigned to start roadside searching. The western side had been divided into sectors and we had been dropped off to check out a 5 mile section.

The road has thin shoulders so walking up the sides you needed to keep an ear open for cars speeding up on you. Rental RV's were their own special threat with inexperienced drivers alternately driving the center line and then hugging the edge. The vehicle's extended mirrors would either crack on coming mirrors or try to take our head off on the roadside.

Looking for clues off the road relied on an attention to detail. You scan the roadside for broken car pieces or a gouged tire track that tracked beyond the sandy road edge. Steep ground needed surveys from multiple angles to check and, occasionally, there would be a need to step down into thicker vegetation to double check for a concealed vehicle.

It was slow progress. Even breaking out of the trees into more rocky ground did not make it easier. The granite offered clearer pathways for longer drops off the road. The edge had a surprising amount of broken glass, car parts and distracting tire prints.

Between us we figured out a system of leapfrogging each other to try and get a complete view of an area. A side chat about POD, Probability of Detection, had us playing with percentages. I would scribble a note on the map. These notes would eventually inform the IC if our assigned area was worth a second look.

The road slipped across the ridge top and started a descent. There was a big pull off and waterfall coming up and it would be a good place to have a break.

Out of nowhere a bear exploded out of the woods right in front of us. It must have missed our stealthy approach until the last moment then sensing trouble it chose to barrel across the road.

Luckily there were no cars speeding by at that moment. With a good head of panicked steam it rocketed up the steep rocky slope to our right.

We both took a moment to marvel at a) the speed b) climbing ability and c)power. The bear was sprint friction climbing slabs and shelves with the dynamic leaps and catches as it powered up and around overhangs. It was amazing.

Then the rocks started coming down.

The bear was clearly taking the opportunity to garden the route. It was dislodging loose rocks and pawing into space. The falling rocks in turn hit others and started a sizable avalanche of material down towards where we were standing.

Rocks started to hit the road, with the really big ones bouncing and making it across to the other side. We scattered out of the way just as a flush of cars appeared.

With rocks in the roadway we waved traffic down and stopped it. The first car in the line wound their window down to ask what was happening.

Looking up slope the bear had paused in its escape. The rock fall had stopped.

"A bear ran across the road and knocked all these rocks down" I said, pointing up to where the bear was standing.

"We are going to have to stop traffic and clear these out the way".

With both lanes stopped we threw the smaller ones off the side before jointly rolling a couple of bigger ones slowly to the edge, then pitching them into a satisfying crashing race downslope.

It took a couple of minutes to clear stuff up.

Returning to the front of the line I told them they were good to go.

The driver paused. He had a question.

"How do you know where to be when this happens?" he asked.

I was confused. I asked him to repeat his question.

He asked again. "How do you know where the bears will be? Where they might knock down rocks?".

The other drivers were getting impatient behind.

I said "Just luck" and waved him on.

Then it clicked what he had been asking.

He had happily been driving along at 55 mph and then suddenly traffic control had been responding to a bear induced rock fall within moments of it happening. He had no idea that we were out looking for a disappeared motorist. He just thought we were out keeping the road open for when the bears decided to block them. And he may still think that to this day.

We never did find the car on our segment. It was spotted from the air miles to the east. Tragically it had failed to make a sharp bend, falling hundreds of feet before hitting talus. Unsurvivable. Bad luck.

THE INITIAL CALL had come at a busy time. The cell signal had been in and out and the call had dropped completely a couple of times. Eventually the IC was able to figure out that someone on the north end of the park was ledged out but stable. With a rough idea of their location the IC told the person to wait, stay safe and we would be up there soon.

In the Valley multiple call outs were happening and the board was filling up as resources were sent out to respond. The IC scrawled a note up with the callers name and location to remind them to keep their eye on it.

Over the afternoon the calls started to stabilize and the IC turned their attention back to the ledged out climber. A helicopter was dispatched to the area to check out what was happening. On the overflight the hoist team chatted about what the scene might look like but were unprepared for what they saw.

Against the backdrop of granite the figure was easy to spot. Facing outward they stood balanced on two small ledges in a slim dihedral. Poised hundreds of feet above the ground they were frozen in place. Strangely their boots laced together hung around their neck.

The crew realized that they would have to move quick. A two person team was lowered onto the face above the trapped man. An anchor was built, and one operator rappelled down to grab and stabilize the subject. The team moved quick to get the man on belay and then up and off the face to safety and a flight back to the cache.

I was in the cache when they arrived. The hoist team walked briskly by on their way to the office with the rescued man in tow. His face was fixed, a thousand yard stare would be the best description.

They spent sometime debriefing and then ushered him back out to the fresh air. He had been hiking and fancied a peak. Spotting the gentle granite ramp he had started walking up towards the top. Subtly the ramp steepened and before he knew it he was starting to slip with his shoes on. Off came his boots and his toes provided the splayed smear to keep moving up. Now it was steep. Trying to down climb out of his predicament he fell twice before arresting his descent in the tenuous position the helicopter had discovered him.

Facing his mortality perched high off the ground he had suddenly remembered his cell phone in his pocket. Taking it out he had managed to make the call that rescued him while staying balanced long enough to ensure a rescue rather than a recovery. His location had risen above the spotty cell coverage in the park and had ensured no mystery was attached to his avoided disappearance. Survivable. Good luck.

THE CHILD HAD WALKED AWAY from their family late the previous afternoon. Just disappeared. The trail was in relatively open country with low bushes and scattered trees. There had been plenty of other visitors but none had seen the 7 year old walking alone. The parents frantic with worry had rechecked the area but realized they needed more help early on. Calling the SAR team the rangers set up containment points, drafted in mutual aid teams and started planning for a big search when the sun came up.

A hundred plus searchers flooded the area in the morning. They started to comb distinct sectors wading through manzanita, checking under fallen logs and exploring rocky crevices a small person could have crawled into. Radios crackled with updates as the command team reviewed reports and examined clues.

Out with the tracker our team looked for a distinct sized sole pattern along the last seen route. Amazingly, despite all the foot traffic, they found the track and traced back and forth on the trail ending up at the parking lot. Checking out the sibling's shoe there was disappointment when we discovered we had successfully tracked the wrong kid.

The parents waited at the IC, an old school bus with radio array, sitting patiently waiting for news. The sibling kicked their heels focussed on not being in the way.

The terrain in the search area was bordered by a road and steep drops off to the Valley below. As teams continued to probe the vegetation and call for the child by name air support arrived to patrol the cliffs and broken ledges. I could hear it buzzing along the rim as we checked the trails for a smaller sized print.

Radio traffic picked up between the helicopter crew and

the IC. They had spotted something and on closer inspection it was our subject. A tiny kid ledged out on a vertical sea of granite.

Just sitting. Not waving, but alive.

Resources got pulled out of the field. Technical gear and team were directed to a specific point. Our team of three were reassigned to the new location. The pace had picked up as we pushed through the manzanita to the lower trail.

More radio conversations led to us to merging with the technical team and starting the steep woody descent down to the cliff edge. Coordinating with the helicopter crew the team leader fine tuned our location above the ledge.

As the climber geared up anchors were secured to trees. The giant trunks gave plenty of monumental points to sling and meet the needs of the lower. Ropes were tied in place. Anchors were checked and double checked with hands on inspections of carabiner gates and knots.

The climber was harnessed up for the drop. A chest mounted radio would help communications during their descent and allow a coordinated raise when they were ready. They crammed some snacks and water into their pack before giving the command to lower.

Slowly they kicked stepped down the leafy ground before stepping out onto the clean granite. They looked over their shoulder eyeing the ledge a 100 feet below and waiting for a reaction from the child.

It does not take long to lower on this terrain. With a safe staging area for the anchors and belay teams the management of the rope was easy. The climber was not hanging in space so they could walk their way down to the ledge. As rescues get more vertical and start to need 1000's of feet of rope the forces demand more involved systems and inherit greater risks.

Quickly the climber gained the ledge and child put out their arms for help. Unhesitatingly they accepted the offer of food and water. No injuries were reported. A quick scan of the area showed how close to a calamity it had been, the ground fell off immediately below the ledge into the unforgiving vertical world Yosemite is world famous for.

The climber tied the child into a harness before clipping them into the rescue rope. Ready to raise.

Reorganizing on top for the raise the team skipped the need for a mechanical advantage system and shifted to simply strong arming the duo back. Staggering ourselves along the ropes length we awaited the command to raise.

Raise.

Grabbing the rope the team started walking and hauling. The power of our collective leg muscles had them at the top in no time. The child seemed unfazed by the operation at the top and released from the system he immediately took off on his own.

As the systems were broken down and ropes coiled responders split off to corral our charge to the top. Forming a rough diamond around them four team members flexed their shape to keep the direction pointing towards home without getting hands on. After a lonely night out on the ledge there was a general consensus to not confuse them with unwanted physical restraint.

Broaching the top of the slope the terrain opened up and at every opportunity the child would detour and make a break for it. Stalled out for a moment by a fallen log on the latest escape bid a team member wordlessly stepped forward and swept them off their feet to perch up on a set of broad shoulders. With no complaint they sat hugging a small stuffed animal and wordlessly accepted their situation.

The walk up the trail was less distracted now and the pace picked up. Team members were elated by the outcome, the optimism had been appropriately pitched.

Breaking out of the trees we could see the parents waiting on the trail, arms outstretched in welcome. Scooping the child from their shoulders and pointing in the direction of the parents the rescuer stood back to watch what would be an emotional reunion. Ignoring their family the child immediately took a right angle turn off the trail and head out on solo expedition again.

We stood back to let the family take over.

Resilience. And luck.

10

WITNESS

D ispatch rang the house and was asking for a hand.

The call was for a CPR in progress down the road. The ambulance was at least 30 minutes out and they had responders coming from both directions but it was still going to be awhile before they were on scene.

Could I head over to the address with oxygen and help out?

I wrote the address down, grabbed my radio, then ran up to the car. The emergency grab bag of oxygen, airways and supplies was already in the vehicle, all I had to do was drive.

The first time I had worked a CPR call was during my emergency room rotation as part of my EMT course. I had used a bag mask while the patient was transported to critical care. When they coded I had been levered out as shocks were administered. It had not left a mark on me. It had felt so surreal to be pumping oxygen into someone as the lift transported them up a floor. It was almost relaxed. But as their vitals pancaked and the electric paddles came out the game changed markedly. By then I was on the margin and had become a detached spectator.

This time was profoundly different.

Arriving at the house full CPR was in process with two people working the stretched out body of the patient with a directed ferocity.

I introduced myself, putting my bags down and gloving up. The CPR team were bathed in sweat, and between breaths and compression gave me a quick overview of what was happening. They were both health care professionals so that explained the effective teamwork and correct technique.

I did a quick scan for pulse and breathing on the patient. Nothing. They looked cyanotic and their body offered little resistance to the forceful chest pounding.

My radio was not working. The battery was flat. Poor planning, again. And no cell signal. In the corner was a telephone with a landline. I did a quick test and got through to Dispatch. Over the line I gave them a quick update on the scene and got an ETA for the team to arrive.

Looking to the side people were slumped on the sofa holding each others hands. The patient's sister and mother watched the CPR in progress quietly. All you could hear was the team counting out the compression breath cycle.

I dropped to my knees at the head. Popping open my bag I rummaged for the mask, flopped out an array of airways and connected up my oxygen.

Telling the team that we had at least another 20 minutes of CPR to go there was a disjointed conversation about airways and oxygen. We decided to just keep going as we were.

I dropped into the rotation. There were little flecks of

vomit around her mouth to clean away. I started breathing. Her name is continuously said. Encouraging her to fight.

Telling her we are here to fight with her.

On the television CPR is a momentary event with crappy compressions, some desperate breaths, a cough and then a magical resuscitation.

That is absolutely not what it is like in real life.

First off it is brutally physical. Even cycling back and fro between breathing and compressions it takes a lot out of you. You rock your weight over locked arms to compress the chest rather than pumping. The rocking is sustained at a high rate rhythm counted out to "Another one bites the Dust" by Queen. The song is happening in your head. The breathing is a steady exhalation and you look for the rise of the chest to ensure it is going in the right way. You start to sweat quick.

Secondly it is sobering. We will have been giving full CPR for over an hour before advanced life support would arrive. In your head you know that there is little hope of bring the patient back but you can't stop as the family battle against that reality. You need to be seen to be doing everything you could. But you know. The way the body presents. The pallor. The lifelessness.

We regularly pause for a moment to check for a pulse or signs of breathing.

Nothing.

Eventually the ambulance crew arrive. They crash in with purpose. Compressions are now shared with more people in the room. The family members administering CPR step back and sit in shocked silence to watch the treatment circus in full swing.

We keep breathing, leads are connected, rhythms sought

and then shocks administered. More analysis. And back to compressions. A bone drill cranks up to start an injection into the shin bone.

Everyone is moving within a focused dance. There are no raised voices. Just a clinical efficiency. People check in with each other in low voices. Everyone is quiet as another round of shocks is administered. No change, no pulse detected.

The paramedic talks to medical control and lays out where the team is at. Control thinks for a moment and then instructs CPR to stop.

Everything goes still. There is moment of silence. Quietly a plan is discussed and I shift position to be with the paramedic as they give the family the death notification. There is a moment of confusion with the deceased's elderly mother as she turns to her daughter and asks "Are they saying she is dead?". The daughter struggles to re -explain what had happened. The mother stares slack jawed at the body now covered by a sheet.

The ambulance crew reassemble for a quick tactical discussion. They pull the lines from the body. Pick up the discarded packaging. They readjust the clothing to cover the patients naked chest.

Sitting with family I start to talk about next steps. The Sheriff is on the way to take over and the funeral home is coming to transport the body to the medical examiner. It's a lot to take in, especially after what they have just witnessed.

I ask if they want time with her before we prepare her for transport. You have to find the right words so I always use the victim's name and help talk them through the options.

They want to say goodbye. I ask for a couple of minutes

and work with medic to tidy up. We fold the sheet down under her chin. Her face gets gently wiped down and hair brushed back. Her eyes are shut. She looks dead. We try to block her head upright but it rest off at an angle. It is the best we can do.

I tell the family we are ready and they come softly forward as we excuse ourselves to hover outside. There is time to compare notes on what happened and how the team did. There is a general agreement that there was not much to be done and that she had been dead before CPR started.

The family wave us back in and I encourage them to look away as we try to get the body into the bag. She is a large person and her build makes it hard to neatly package. All of us are bent over trying to get purchase so we lift, then slide the open bag under her.

Count of three and we have her up and then in. The sound of the zip has a sad finality to the evening. Her body stowed out in the entrance wayout of sight. The sheriff arrives and takes over. I transition the family to his care. They are tearful and exhausted. The sister decides to reach out to the deceased's family. A raw early morning call no one wants to make or receive.

A final check in with the crew and I am back in the car for the short drive home. These things stay with you. My shower feels like more of a ritual than a need. I am trying to wash the emotions, smells and textures away but they are going to persist. The mother's uncomprehending stare at the body of her daughter will always be with me. A holiday flipped in a moment to a horror day.

Though I cannot recall her name, every time I drive by the house I remember her. I see her family in the wings waiting for the miracle. The three of us frantically trying to pump life into her body. I hear Medical Control confirming what we all knew. I remember preparing the body for viewing. The final zip of the bag.

It is another haunting.

11

ROADKILL

The first speeding ticket (42mph in a 25 mph zone) was the result of marveling. Chapel Straight in the Valley is the first really great view of Yosemite Falls. On this morning it was spectacular. I was still pretty new to the park so glancing out to the left I was stunned to see the Falls in full flow, but more impressive was the giant snow cone at its base. I had not seen the phenomenon before. A steep sided icy mass rising hundreds of feet up to meet the crashing falling water took my breath away.

I let out an audible profanity of wonderment.

This was followed immediately by another type of profanity when the flashing blue lights of a Ranger car lit up behind me and I had to pull over.

I knew the Ranger, his wife worked with me.

The stop was professional. We kept it formal without first names. I got a lecture about speeding killing animals and I pled distraction using the snow cone as a mitigation. I got a ticket, was late for work and made organizational amends by not collecting mileage reimbursement for a year.

I made amends to the Federal Government by paying

the $25 ticket immediately and apologizing in person to the Chief Ranger for being a terrible role model to staff.

The second ticket was a soft one, and Mike, if you are out there, you know it was too. The Wawona Tunnel on the south side of the Valley was a daily part of my commute. Nearly a mile long it is straight and well lit it giving you a chance to speed things up. Mid point along the tunnel is a small pullout where maintenance can access the giant fans that keep the air moving. Historically this provided some storage for emergency supplies during the Cold War as the tunnel was designated a nuclear fallout shelter for the park employees.

Unbeknown to me this was a favorite pullout for some Rangers to catch speeders. Interestingly not all the Rangers agreed on the ethics of this ticket, unfortunately on this day Mike did.

I was running late for a river day and so had to pick the pace up. My 4x4 was distinct as it had a brightly colored whitewater canoe strapped to the roof rack like a teal flavored missile. I half registered Mike's car as I raced by and then really noticed it as his flashers came on and I had to pull over. Again.

We kept it professional. No first names. ID produced. Words spoken, avoid killing animals mentioned, and ticket written. ($75 this time). There was a brief haggle over my speed. Initially Mike proposed I was doing over seventy, but we bargained it down to a more acceptable 56mph.

Ironically I was speeding in the tunnel because after my first ticket I had started scientifically researching where animals got killed and if speed did play a part. And my research to that point has indicated animals were not getting run over in the tunnel.

My regular commute provided a twice a day data collection opportunity. Jeffrey gave me an NPS metal notebook holder, the same type used to write my tickets on. Dropping in maps and some poorly formatted tables I would record all the dead critters observed on the drive.This allowed me to plot where I observed flattened fauna and start to paint a picture about other factors that might have led to the untimely demise of each one.

I created a handful of acronyms to guide my observations.

SPLAT.

Species. Perseverance and PALS. Location. Appearance. Time.

I got proficient at identifying species fairly quickly. Grey Squirrels had a bushy quality and their tails often survived the most devastating hit to indicate what they had been. Some I could speed by, but other more smeared remains needed me to pull over and poke at them to find teeth, or feet, to have an accurate identification. I once recognized a merganser by their feet alone after a car did a real number on the body.

Perseverance and PALS. The length of time that the dead bodies stayed around was an ancillary part of the study. Turned out that the ravens and coyotes actively patrolled the roads checking out for free meals. Within minutes certain roadkill would attract a scavenging fan club. These opportunists (PALS -Predators Acquiring a Light Snack) had more road sense and rarely figured in my statistics.

Certain Determined Cadavers (CDCs) had been so badly smooshed that they were formed part of the road bed. Even the most focused raven gave up picking at these and only the advent of the winter snowplowing would ultimately move them.

Location. Location. Location. Within weeks kill zones emerged. Squirrels were getting hammered near pullouts and campsites. Acceleration and overtaking locations seemed to indicate higher speeds led to more deaths.

I utilized my own grading system for Appearance. The Appearance Index Matrix, or AIM for short. I attached a number after each fatality was surveyed.

1 – victim appears to sleeping in poorly chosen location

2 – clear dent but generally easily recognized

3 - victim clearly exploded

4 – victim resembles badly molded pancake

5 – victim effectively disassembled and spread liberally around area

Time. I was trying to establish if there was difference between early or late surveys but statistically there was not much in it.

I had been happily quietly conducting the survey when I was asked by the Wildlife Biologist if I would like to present my findings at the monthly science talk, The Croaking Toad. Of course I said yes but in order to be official I had to complete and submit a research permit. Reviewing the application I saw I had listed getting tickets as being one of my qualifications!

Permit in hand I needed to work on the presentation.

"SPLAT goes the Weasel" was the final product. It was centered on the premise that although flattened they were not forgotten. I created a podium for species that were particularly good at getting run over, Grey Squirrels were the gold medalists. I labelled the top three ROUS, Rodents of Unusual Slowness.

The audience was larger than expected. Some people came early to get a front row seat. I had brief moment questioning if my power point was little too relaxed but it was too late to change anything. I had started down the road of a parody science presentation but somewhere along the way it transitioned to something with a core message. By the presentation's end I had rolled out a message that speed kills, information could change behaviors and that maybe the Park could do something.

Red Bear, Dead Bear was born.

At first there had been a discussion about a pirate campaign of stenciling giant red bear outlines on the roads wherever a bear had been hit. I had tried simply spray painting roadkill in place before shoveling them off the road but the finer points of the anatomy did not show up. It just turned into a neon circle of paint with an asphalt blob in the middle.

The stencil idea would have been great but too many people knew about it so I was going to get stitched up as an organic Banksy. On top of that someone told me that it was not permitted under Federal Highway codes so we shifted to a legal route. The initial signs were small 8 inch squares with a red bear outline.

Tori and I hung them up on a dumpster and drove by them at different speeds trying to ascertain if they would be noticed. The answer was that at 60 mph on a dumpster they were not. A different approach was needed.

Fortunately Adrienne took the project over and successfully followed through on codes. She got giant Red Bear, Dead Bear signs approved. Wildlife management set them out at locations where bears had been hit to try to influence drivers to slow down. Visitors liked them so much that they would steal them and NPS had to start locking them to something heavy and immovable when they were set out.

∼

DRIVING friends over the Tioga Road the bear was spotted lying by the road's edge. Pulling over, we walked stealthily back to check on it. There was no obvious blood. There was no breathing but to be sure I tapped its open eye to see if there was a reflective blink.

Nothing.

Cars sped by as usual, racing to whatever important view needed to be photographed or trail to be hiked. Locals are the worst, a strange entitlement to get their quicker than everyone else premised on the phrase, I live here.

Such a pathetic excuse.

Getting there quicker has a cost.

We rarely bear it.

They do.

∽

12

FLOATER

"Hey Dad. Whats this?"

It had just been a normal hike along the river bank until they discovered the finger. After an initial panic the dad phoned their discovery in and the rangers responded. The finger was bagged, placed on ice.

The Valley was packed with visitors so if the body was out there someone would likely see it. The finger sat in its bag in incident command waiting for dispatch to the medical examiner.

After strategizing the IC called out for Swiftwater techs to conduct a float and search. Grabbing gear and river boards they headed upstream, before launching and slowly probing the pools and riffles while foot patrols checked the banks and margins.

Visitors sensed something was going on and started to ask questions. Some of their inquiries were deflected, others were given the briefest overview of the circumstances. Putting your head underwater was a good technique to avoid getting drawn into extended conversation.

Slowly the search teams floated and walked their way downstream. Masks and snorkels in the clear shallow water ensured that there was a high probability of detection for more body parts or clues. The banks are well travelled so it seemed inconceivable that more clues had not been stumbled upon.

It was a hot day so the river searchers were enjoying the cool water and lazy float. Periodic check ins on the radio on their position confirmed nothing had been found.

The Search and Rescue Cache attracted fly-bys from rangers during lulls in their shift. They could wander into the Command room and eye the dry erase board, look at the incident log and draw up a chair to chat with the crew when the radio traffic allowed.

On this occasion the ranger caught up on the incident and got a chance to consider the search assignments. Eyeing the bag of ice they asked if it contained the finger? Affirmative the Incident Commander replied.

Can I take a look?

Be my guest.

Unfolding the top the ranger splayed the bag open. They carefully pushed the ice to one side, revealing the finger.

Intently they considered the body part. They reached in and rolled it to look at the other side. A pause.

It's not a finger they said.

What?

It's a chicken gizzard they said.

Confirmed by further investigation the team were summoned back to base. Looking for more of the chicken seemed pointless.

∾

RESPONDING you can feel overdressed on scene. This was one of those occasions. High summer with the river pooled out with minimal flow families set up with deckchairs and coolers on the beaches as kids plunge about, safe from being washed away. Lots of sunscreens and beach casual, no shoes.

The SAR team rolled up to respond to an incapacitated swimmer on the far bank. Policy dictated helmets and PFD's so an excess of equipment was distributed to the team. Skipping the wetsuit we waded then swam when our floatation made walking impossible. Our patient was curled up in the fetal ball whimpering as they tried to manage their dislocated shoulder pain.

Checking in, and overcoming the language barrier, there was a confirmation of the shoulder as being the only injury. All that was needed was to transport them over the narrow watery band to the ambulance.

The patient was reluctant to move. They had established a place to manage the pain and were disinterested in exploring the deeper pain that movement suggested. We shelved the plan of putting them in the water and towing them over. It was not going to happen.

Pointing at the ambulance crew on the beach we explained that a few feet away pain medications and shoulder reduction were available. Still the patient expressed disinterest in moving. Thinking on our feet we spied a child's raft ashore and requested to use it. The family were more than happy to provide a prop for the home movie they had been shooting.

Now equipped with a brightly colored inflatable we had an easier evacuation tool. But still our patient would not move. It was time for executive action. They presented as a neat bundled ball so it was easy to sweep them up and pivot them aboard the raft. Supported in the slightly deflated wrap of the raft, they murmured rude words in a foreign language, but were already on their way to a medicated numbness so I discounted it as pain induced and did not take it personally.

With a quick transfer to the ambulance and a stabilized position they seemed happier. But not as happy as the family we had borrowed the raft from. They treated its return like a holy relic. They chatted through what they had filmed, how excited they had been and how happy they were to have been part of the team.

Their kids returned to the water with the raft and began recreating the incident. Taking turns they slipped off the bank into the raft's embrace to be rescued again and again. I am not sure if they used the rude words but they were laughing a lot when we left them.

I wonder how they tell their version of the story when they look at the video. I hope they remember the laughter rather than the pain. The thrill of rescuing another. That their tiny raft was the key to the mission. And that a game, borne of helping others, extended into their adult lives.

∽

13

SPLASH

Arriving I could see the car passengers on the sidewalk next to the ambulance. A shivering group with blankets across their shoulders huddled together.

Their car was in the middle of the river, fully submerged. The roof was just visible at the surface. Walking to the river edge it was clear where they had crashed through a wooden barrier, threaded the needle between two trees and then vaulted into the water. Somehow they had avoided wrecking headfirst into rocks and trees to find the safest landing spot.

A quick scene assessment and I was gearing up for a dip. I decided to swim into the car from the lower side. That way potential snag points could be avoided and the bail out options were unobstructed downstream.

A check of the gear. Wetsuit zipped, pfd snugged, safety line secured. I grabbed a window punch, a dull pointed stabbing tool for breaking out the glass. A quick check-in helmet bump to my belayer and I was flat diving into the river.

The water was flowing deep but not too quick so it was easy to ferry into the downstream eddy the car had created. Pulling up on the hood I could see the front window was unbroken and could step up safely onto the roof.

Signaling I was ok to the shore team I noticed the excess safety line looped downstream haphazardly. The belayer drew it in, tight enough to know where it was, but not too tight to impede my movement.

Twenty minutes had passed since the car went in. A head count by the passengers had indicated that they had all got out. A quick survey found just one window open, the rear passenger side. All the doors appeared shut. The inside still needed to be checked.

Leaning over the side sticking my head under water I peered in. The water was clear enough to see that there were no bodies inside. That was a relief. Surfacing I shouted the car looked clear while making the mental note to bring a snorkel and mask next time.

It was impressive that five of them had got out of the car and swum ashore. None of the doors were open and just one window. I am not sure how they did it. Accidents can really accelerate survival reflexes.

The crowd on the bridge had grown. Plenty of spectators today. Fortunately they would not have to see a body recovery. Any action like this attracts a crowd. I wondered if they had any good pictures?

The car needed to be retrieved. A thin oil sheen was building in the downstream eddy and the smell of fuel was in the air.

Time to start breaking windows. With the rear passenger window open already it made sense to punch out the corner of the back window and pass the cable around the rear post. It was one of the strongest points on the car.

Grasping the punch I dropped to my knees and tried to get purchase on the slippery roof. The water sheen left me skating and the only place to grab was the top of the passenger door with my left hand. My arm made a few practice swings with the tool, measuring the distance and picking the best spot. The punch needed to drop into the corner, with minimal follow through.

A few more swings and then it was time to go.

BAM! It was more Splash than Bam.

An air explosion geysered out of the hole and the car started to resettle on the bottom. As it rocked side to side I unclipped from the safety line and prepared to dive out and away. It felt like it was going to flip.

Still on the roof with my heart racing the car settled down, a little deeper, and stopped rocking.

I grinned stupidly at the shore crew. The car was nowhere near flipping. It was just trapped air finding a way out and scaring me silly.

A rope was thrown out to ferry the towing cable to the car. The heavy steel hawser was easy to thread through the broken back window and after fishing around in the interior I was able to grab it and fix it back on itself. Coordinating with the tow driver the cable was gently snugged down. Once sure that it would stay in place I could swim back to shore.

Tensioned cable brings its own dangers. The shore team took a big step backwards to watch while making sure that there were trees in the way should it snap and vengefully snake itself towards us.

Slowly the cable torqued the car around, gradually spinning and dragging it out of the water. As the car broke the surface the wipers swung back and forwards across the windscreen. It seemed abit late.

The passengers were still around the ambulance. Although one of them was on a stretcher now. The tone of the interactions with the rangers had changed. Turned out that the driver minutes before the accident had already got a speeding ticket on El Cap straight. When he was confronted now with what appeared to be another case of dangerous driving he suddenly developed neck pain and decided to stop being asked questions by lying down on a gurney groaning. I never found out if this evasive strategy was successful.

I SPENT a long day in the Valley working with a crew setting up the largest redirection of traffic in the park's history. The Yosemite traffic snarl ups are a thing of legend and this work was the culmination of two years of planning.

Locals were recruited to push barriers into place delineating new traffic lanes, shutting off poor road connections and all the time maintaining traffic flow and pedestrian access. There were front loaders moving around junctions shifting in K-Bar for barricades, while a water tanker filled them up to give them more heft against collisions.

As the traffic slowly passed through work zones we answered questions, helped visitors get oriented and dealt with over entitled locals chipping in with their wisdom with unhelpful regularity.

It was an amazing ten hours of positioning and fine tuning as we adapted to the needs of buses and distracted drivers. Finally an hour before sunset the closures were pulled and the system fully opened. It was wonderful to see previous bottlenecks open up and traffic start to flow more freely.

I had had an interesting distraction in the afternoon when a visitor dressed in a lifejacket and soaking wet asked me if I had a hook he could use to rescue his phone from the river. As he explained what he needed it became clear he actually had lost both his and his friend's phones when their raft capsized. After 30 minutes of frigid searching he had found them but they were too deep to retrieve.

I tried getting some support from the Search and Rescue cache but they had a rescue happening and could not spare anyone. So after a quick chat with the crew boss I grabbed my farmer john (a sleeveless wetsuit), my mask and snorkel then headed off to see what I could do.

As we walked to the river bank I was asked if I was a Manchester United supporter - they had noticed the Chevrolet brand on my shirt and connected to the sponsor of United. I declared I was a proud Aston Villa supporter and out of nowhere they started to recite the lineup for the early 80's Villa team that won the European Cup - Morley, Shaw, Withe etc. I could not believe it - they laughed and talked about how they had watched games with their dads and I talked about going to games with my dad! Inspired by the Brummie (a person from Birmingham, England) connection I was fired up to recover their phones.

At the water's edge I surveyed the scene and chatted with them where the phones were. I pulled up one of the shoulder straps and it snuggly snapped into place, backed up by velcro. Unfortunately while securing the other shoulder the first strap failed and I found myself alternating between the two as I tried to keep them both in place and ultimately failing. The pandemic disruption has added a few pounds and the stretchy challenge for the wetsuit was too much so I entered the water bare chested wearing a pair of neoprene leggings.

The water was brisk but three dives later I had got the phones and made my way to shore. The guys were ecstatic and being new phones they were waterproof and still worked. A quick round of high fives and I jogged off and back to work on the traffic detail.

An hour later one of them returned on his bike to say thank you and take a picture of me and asked for my boss's name so he could send a note. He was still excited and happy to have his phone back.

He left with a deeper commitment to support Villa.

As I was about to leave 3 hours later they both turned up this, time with one of their mothers. She wanted to have a picture taken with me. So there we were with a backdrop of the Yosemite Falls when the final twist was revealed. Being in tech the guys did everything with their phones, including as it turned out getting their car to work. Without the phone recovery they would have been stranded.

THE PHONE CALL from the Bear Management team was asking for help. They needed assistance recovering a radio telemetry collar from a drowned bear they found in the river. Tori, the wildlife biologist, had recognized the unique challenges of the job and called me in.

The bear was jammed up below a small drop. Head pointed up stream the carcass had been stripped clean of fur by the flow and only a small bloated island of flesh poked above the water. This helped to manage the pungency of death plus the super cold water had helped to preserve the body from the worst ravages of decomposition.

Given the position of the body it was impossible to see if a radio collar was still on the bear's neck from the shore. The height of the bank and water flow made it difficult and potentially dangerous to probe any further from above.

Access was restricted – steep water polished boulders on each side of the squeeze made it difficult to climb down without needing to step on the body, something I was reluctant to do. After a quick survey it was decided that a downstream assault would be best. The current over and under the body seemed manageable and I thought I would be able to visually assess if the radio collar was in place from the water.

After a quick change on the bank I climbed down to the river and double checked my equipment. Zips fully engaged, shoes velcro'd shut, fins snapped on my heels, snorkel and mask in hand.

Stepping into the current the sharp cold of snow melt was instantly registered. Moving deeper I paused at mid thigh to prepare my mask, a quick spit and rub of the glass then a rinse before snugging it all in place. Casting an eye upstream I again assessed the approach – a steady stream of air bubbles provided a pathway to the bear.

I eased into the shoulder deep water, experience had taught me to take a minute to adjust to the chill before moving. The slow immersion allowed me to control breathing and focus on what needed to be done in the moving water.

A final glance up at the bank at Tori, and then in I plunged.

A couple of driving strokes and kicks later and I was behind the bear – the entrapped bloated corpse created a sizable mid stream eddy to stall out in, something I took advantage of to adjust my mask and snorkel as I hovered just below the surface. Looking upstream the hulking mass cast a dark impenetrable shadow on the river bottom – I realized that my plan of swimming under the body to look for the collar was not going to work without an unpleasant ursine embrace.

This is when it became clear that all was not as it had seemed from the bank. The "air bubble" train I had noted from the shore had undergone a subtle change in the water – it was still a train but was made up pure bear fat. And a tremendous amount of bear fat particles – a positive slick in fact.

And I was in the middle of it.

Looking down I could see particles attaching themselves to my wetsuit. Holding my hand out the ghost white globules happily secured themselves to my fingers.

It was slowly dawning on me that I was bathing in a steady stream of decomposing bear grease.

Popping to the surface I conveyed the assessment of the situation – the collar dive was a no go and I was covered in bear grease. There is a clear picture in my mind of Tori's delighted facial expression upon the news I was fully immersed in a giant river of fat. I am pretty sure she laughed out loud.

Abandoning my cholesterol rich eddy I struck out for the bank, unfortunately taking a couple of gulps of water after I forgot to put my snorkel back in after my shore report. Emerging from the shallows it was clear that every square inch of my frame was dotted with white flecked globules that resisted any attempt to brush them off.

There is not much you can do under these circumstances so I just wrapped myself in a towel and sought a hot shower to clean up. And lots of soap.

14

TRIAGE

DEF. ASSIGN DEGREES OF URGENCY TO
(WOUNDED OR ILL PATIENTS).

S ki Patrolling at Badger Pass was more about being an EMT that could ski than Skier with EMT skills. The oldest ski area in California and one of only two remaining ski areas in a US National Park Badger has 700 vertical feet at its highest point and a seven and half minute lift ride to the top.

On an icy morning with fresh corduroy the slopes are bulletproof for first runs so I could point my tips straight and missile to the bottom with no danger of hitting anyone or thing. Skiing the boundaries and checking the bamboo could wait for half an hour on super cold mornings. Always racing the minute hand to break 60 seconds to the bottom.

Badger Pass was a 15 minute drive from the house so it was easy to turn up for patrol when they needed an extra hand at short notice. The terrain was not technical, there was rarely a lift line and you could cheaply ski all day.

As a ski patroller it was low key. No avalanche chutes to manage, the occasional dangerous skier with nowhere left to run getting caught at the lift line. Locals storming the resort and skipping buying a pass. That was a classic as the ski manager when he confronted them was accused of profiling. He agreed he was, but he was only profiling local people without a ticket.

There are plenty of secret powder stashes after the storms. On slow days the crowds could fail to materialize due to road closures, leading to curious exploration of the trees and abandoned runs. There were surprises each season to rediscover.

The radio call was for a high speed collision on the beginner slope. The slope angle is so low you can skate ski up if you have to. I skied over the top, ripped down to the scene and snapped off my skies to began my assessment. When I say snapped off my skis I actually went through a two step process with my tele bindings, first unclipping the heel and then a fiddle with the safety clip, before flipping the ski and stamping the binding into the snow. A good reason why most slopes do not let you tele ski on patrol.

Area accidents tended to pulse up in the afternoon as the classes ended and beginners began to push the boundaries of their perceived skills and the reality of their actual level of proficiency. You could see them tackling steeper stuff with a level of panicked desperation as the speed increased exponentially and their control shrank to zero. Sometimes in anticipation of the consequence of the oncoming disaster they would become masters of their domain and initiate a rapid shut down crash. Hats, gloves and glasses would fly off and they would yard sale their way to a sliding stop. Slowly they would reassemble themselves to either try another sliding tiptoe between survival and disaster. Or they would pick their gear up and stumble their way to the flats.

If they rolled the dice and adventure came up then they would inadvertently use other techniques. The arrowed high speed boundary fence envelopment might see them destroying a few bamboo poles but the cushioned snaring impact of the snow fence muted the damage. Trees could alarmingly decelerate them either by sweeping them off their feet with a bough under their arms. Or by instantaneously stopping them with their contact with an immovable object.

I had responded to a variant on these. Two skiers moving at speed had collide and in the ensuing physics equation had bounced violently out of their skis, goggles and hats into separate wheezy heaps.

As the first patroller on scene I did a quick visual assessment and called for more patrollers. There was more groaning than talking from both parties so I was glad when back up arrived.

We split to do our initial assessments. Checking the majors I scanned for airway, breathing and a pulse. With such a violent witnessed collision and wreckage it was safe to assume there was sufficient force and mechanism for a back injury so spinal precautions kicked in.

Asking for permission and getting a breathless assent I did my hands on check and started to scan for blood. No signs of bleeding out. I moved on to a more focussed examine for points of tenderness, things out of alignment and obvious angulation. The patient was complaining of pain on their right side and between labored inhalations made it clear they were struggling to breath. There was so much distracting pain I was not sure they could be trusted when asked if there was any loss of consciousness. I finished up my initial survey and contacted the other patroller.

"What have you got?" I asked.

"Full recall of events, no loss of consciousness, lots of

pain in their shoulder but nowhere else. Vitals slightly elevated". They replied.

"What about you?"

"Mine can't breath"

"Ok in the world of triage you win lets pack them up and crank the oxygen"

Triage is the tool used to assess who is the most seriously injured and needs the most urgent care. Not being able to breath is a fundamental need so my patient won the right to be packaged first in the sled for transport.

Keeping the spinal precautions in place we did a rapid transfer and flashed them down the hill to the clinic. The high flow oxygen helped somewhat with their oxygen saturation but their pain remained high.

Once in the warmth of the clinic the nurse did a more thorough assessment. More oxygen but still under spinal precautions so the patient was in a collar and on the back board. Not easy to get a position of comfort.

More calls were coming off the hill and now we had patients on every chair and one on the floor. I wanted to hang out and confirm my assessment with the nurse but they were already calling in the ambulance and scribbling notes. Looking them over I could see the cause for concern, busted ribs and a punctured lung. The patient was going to be uncomfortable for awhile.

Adjusting my goggles, snapping my helmet back on I headed out for the next pickup. Lifts shut at 4pm and so thirty more minutes of skiing left, plenty of time for more disaster.

～

15

DRESSED TO SURVIVE

The Search and Rescue Cache was not a particularly impressive building. As with so many NPS buildings what they were yesterday does not limit how they are used today or what might be their future tomorrow.

The cache was no different. Awkward connections had people's desks set up in the connecting corridors. The Command room was just a place where the doors could be shut and quiet conversations could happen with less interruptions.

The cache was its normally hive of activity in the summer. SAR team members were grabbing gear and snacks. Command staff were walking back and fro looking busy. The Fed Ex delivery guy was looking for someone to sign for something.

Today was the first full day of a search for a missing college student. They had been part of a group trip in the north west corner of the park and had been reported missing earlier in the day. There was some confusion about what exactly had happened. The first reports had talked about the student being missing for a few hours. The rest of the group had spent the morning and early afternoon looking for them but had picked up no clues. Only after this drew a blank they decided to contact SAR.

A search was scaled up and ground teams dispatched to the area with helicopter overflights planned. The investigators began a more detailed interview of the group. The story began to take a different angle. With directed questioning the group leader changed their story. The student had been missing for much longer. They had been missing for more than 24 hours, having disappeared the previous evening.

Why they had hidden this did not matter for now. What mattered was to reexamine the potential area to search, the subject had had 12 more hours to move than previously thought.

My assignment was to work with the college and family to keep them informed of the operation and answer their questions. Most searches start with optimism and hope. You are focussed on interviewing, finding clues and getting boots on the ground. With good weather and survivable terrain you can have optimism as a searcher.

But we were more than 24 hours in on this one and no clues had sprung up. Listening to the group's decision making and hearing the investigator talk about the student started to reduce the sense of optimism and hope I had. There was more than a hint that drugs might be involved and the place last seen was right next to a deep cold lake.

Internally I began to have reservations about whether this was going to work out for the best.

Then they handed out the missing person's photograph and description of their clothing.

I immediately felt better.

The image was of a scraggly haired student. He looked wild, better yet feral. And his clothes. A sleeveless plaid shirt and cut off jean shorts. His footwear were a plastic overshoe with the individual toe fingers. It was a fantastically ill-equipped ensemble for being lost above 8000 feet in the Sierras.

The group agreed while the scenario was serious the character was the type that survived this type of ordeal.

Talking with the family and college as time went by I remained genuinely optimistic about locating them. The weather was mild. There was plenty of water in the area and with increased helicopter flights we were able to cover a large area with reasonable hope of spotting him if he was still alive.

Day three of the search rolled around and an afternoon overflight spotted the missing person. They looped the area and chose a landing spot down hill of them. As the helicopter landed with its rotors low on the uphill side the missing person ran down towards the rescue team. Only a timely intervention of frantic waving stopped them from running into the rotor which would have been a messy end to what was an ultimately a happy outcome.

COMMUTING out of the Valley each day I got in the habit of leaving my radio on, at least until I started the climb up to the tunnel. You could listen in to the traffic of the wildlife crews coming on shift or an unlucky tourist rolling a stop sign before getting pulled over. Fire briefs would detail moisture and weather. The distinct tones for callouts would break through to alert fire, SAR or medical teams to specific incidents.

As I crossed Pohono Bridge the SAR tone went out. A quick blast and then details. Swiftwater response. Bridalveil.

I was two minutes away. It is not a good thing to free-lance a response. You wait to assigned rather than just showing up on the scene. You need to respect the hierarchy of the ICS and allow a planned response to play out.

On this occasion I figured that I could roll by the reporting unit in the parking lot and check and see if they needed me. Glancing in the back of the car I could see my pfd and a helmet. I was equipped.

In the parking lot the reporting unit agreed I could join in. There were a limited number of experienced Swiftwater technicians in the park so to have one on scene was advantageous. I got told to gear up.

Snugging the car up against the dumpster I jumped out and rummaged in the back for my gear. As I flipped stuff over I realized that my pfd and my helmet were the only bits of equipment I had. The rest of it was drying at my house.

Pulling the pfd on and clipping my helmet to the shoulder strap I started running up the trail. My speed was limited as I was wearing flip flops, the only pair of shoes I had. Jogging around tourists I caught up some other responders and together we picked our way up the trail. As the trail petered out we scrambled up the rocks and slabs to the accident scene.

Traversing below a steep slab we arrived at the staging area. It was a bit chaotic. A responder sat out on the edge of sharp drop. They were shouting instructions to someone below in the water. Back in the creek bed a group of friends crowded the space, taking turns to move to the cluttered edge to engage their friend below.

I pushed forward through them to find out what the plan was. A uniformed ranger turned up and command presence got exercised on the friend group. They stepped back and stayed out the way.

With more space you could see what had happened. Their friend playing near the edge had slipped into the deep pool below. The combination of an overhang, water polished granite and physical limitations had trapped them in their frigid prison. The water was too deep to stand up in and the sun was barely tickling the far wall.

It looked cold.

The friend by now had swum over to the downstream part of the pool. They were trying to warm themselves up so had hauled out on the hot rocks uncomfortably close to the next drop. I shouted over for them to move back towards the water, but faced with the cool shadows or toasty rocks they had little interest in complying. And I did not have much command presence dressing in shorts, flips flops and no shirt.

The on scene IC laughed when he looked at my outfit but it was all he had so over the edge I went. Hand over hand I climbed down the rope before dropping the last few feet into the water. It was as cold as it looked. You could see why the victim was perched out in the sun. Swimming over there was a realization how lucky he had not gone over a few weeks before. Then rather than grounding out on the lip he would have just washed over into a fatal drop.

I made contact with him. No injuries, but his efforts to escape had exhausted him so he was not in much shape to help himself up the rope. The team was going to have to haul him up.

I pulled some webbing out of my pfd and quickly visually established that it was going to be insufficient to the task. The victim was a larger person and was going to need a much longer piece of webbing. The team above dropped me more supplies and I started building a body harness. Given their size I needed to tie a sit and chest harness - the combination would reduce the risk of the victim getting inverted during the raise.

Even with all the webbing it still was a snug fit. As he stood up the webbing settled and he maintained a slight stooped posture to avoid undue pressure to his groin. I tied him in and started explaining for a final time what we were going to do. Float him across the pool and then raise him up the slick waterfall chute he had pitched off an hour before. As a final gesture I strapped a pfd around him, at least he would not sink on the way over.

His responses were hampered by the tightness of the harness but his grunts were taken as approvals. The belay team pulled in the slack and we both entered into the deeper water. He looked worried as the rope team pulled him in, his jaw clenched but that might have been due to the ungodly squeeze of the harness. Due to the restrictive nature of the harness he found it difficult to swim so I towed him on his back into position.

He was facing the wall now. The rope above had tightened and his breathing had become a little labored as the improvised harness uncomfortably fully loaded. His hands splayed across the polished rock pushing outward. Most of him was still below the surface.

Treading water beside him I gave him some encouraging words and told him it would be over soon. The team began to haul him up. His weight was a challenge and the team could only make small incremental bouncing gains. This probably did not help his overall comfort as the each stop was a trifle jarring as the haul system was reset. The grunting was now replaced by regular deep exhalations each time the hauling stopped.

At one point I swam below to push him up a little higher but deadlifting under water was both taxing and ineffective so that approach was abandoned. The lift took a few minutes before he was able to reach up to the lip where the team reached over to grab his harness before rolling him over the edge.

All that was left was for me to exit the pool. Sweeping the area for any lost items I swam back one last time and grabbed the rope. The ascent was now not only polished but wet. Probably a bare foot ascent was best. Flip flops off and stuffed in my pfd I reached high up the rope and began to hand over hand climb. The rock was unhelpful and soon it was all about my arms but it was only a few feet to go before I topped out.

Flip flops back on I grabbed my dry shirt and stepped out into the sun. Dressed to survive. And rescue.

~

16

EMBARRASSED AND COLD

S wimming out to the island I realized that my suit had not been vented. I was so excited to get in the water and rescue someone I had forgotten to push the excess air out of the dry suit. My arms and shoulders ballooned as I paddled the river board making it hard to move my arms effectively.

The spectators on the bridge had a great view of the action. Two early season rafters had flipped and managed to maroon themselves midstream. Having got justifiably scared by the river speed and low temperatures they decided to just wait to be rescued. They had shouted for help to passerby's and SAR had responded within minutes.

As soon as my feet touched the bottom the neck gasket was eased open. Sinking down in the water the air was squeezed out and the suit now shrink wrapped around my body. The victims were happy to see me. But their enthusiasm was muted by being thoroughly soaked through.

Looking up at the bridge I nodded my head at the peanut gallery. They had let out a round of applause when I grounded on the island and had their cameras out to capture developments.

"Are you feeling a little embarrassed?" I offered.

"And cold" one of them replied.

Not wanting to extend the conversation into how they got there and what they had learned from the experience I got them ready for evacuation.

A rescue rope was transferred to the rigged sling off the front handles of the river board and the shore crew signaled they were ready to haul. Slipping off to the down stream side of the board I motioned to get on of them on the board. They stepped into the water and reached forward and grabbed the board's handles. Their chest were up and out of the water, I could reach over their hips and grab the opposite side handle locking them in place. A quick signal to the shore and the load line started hauling them across. My job was to keep them on the board, keep the upstream side high so the current did not grab it and flip us over. A quick drop off, rope shuffle and then back over to get the other rafter. No problem on the pick off and another quick retrieve. After less then 15 minutes in the water I was chilling down so there was no hanging about debrief. A quick bank side strip down and I was getting toasty in my dry clothes.

MOST OF THE rescues had an element of luck and easy extraction. And they tended to happen in the same locations. One summer there were so many rescues from the same spot that is became known as the Usual Spot, aka Shipwreck Island. The SAR team ended up just camping out on the bank as it was easier than dispatching on busy days.

At Mirror Lake there is a deceptive rocky ledge that appears to offer an easy crossing point between trails. Visitors would commonly start the traverse, then someone would lose their footing and wash down the rocky chutes. If they stayed in the flow they would have a painful butt bumping ride into a pool and could self rescue. Most of the incidents SAR responded to were midstream standings. They would be sitting just off the shore at the top of the rapid on a cluster of rocks. They were normally stable enough to not worry too much about them so on turning up on scene a technician would start talking to them while the rest of the crew would start the response.

Coming from a traditional rigging background SAR leadership remain committed to large amounts of knots, anchors and directional forces. A ladder would be rigged to be lowered out to the stranded party but the angles and loads often meant that the last part of the lower was not particularly controlled. There was always the potential that the ladder in the last few feet of descent would crash onto the victim compounding their predicament with a head injury.

Spotting a perfectly situated flat rock there was a realization that the ladder could be deployed in a horizontal position without any rigging. Lining the ladder up with midstream location the largest SAR members stood on the lower ladder section, weighing it down. A small responder would then shoot the upper extension out, firing it over the divide to complete the bridge over the water.

Deployment took seconds. No one had to climb a tree and best of all no victim was pushed off their safe rock into the water by an out of control ladder.

And to the surrounding crowds it looked much more professional.

It was straight forward to monkey across the rungs and drop into the eddy behind the rock. From there you could get a pfd on the victim and coach them back across the rungs to the shore. Hovering downstream of the ladder it could be steadied by a bracing hip. If anyone ended up in the water it was an easy launch to try and grab them.

WATER RESCUE initially has a chaotic deployment nature. Radio traffic would convey a sense of urgency with just a mention of people in the water. Units would self deploy and as resources flooded the area the Incident Commander on the ground would need to exert control quickly before things got out of hand. Once the incident was understood, single adult stable on a rock or child disappeared on fast flowing water 15 minutes ago, then resources could be more efficiently directed.

Water has a deceptive quality on SAR. Bundled up in the gear with high flotation and a helmet on everyone looks like they know what they are doing. The redundancy present in rock rescue with defined edges, belayed exposure and ruthless technical management mean novices have an almost automatic back up. In Swiftwater rescuers can turn up with little more than a three day training to their name and zero personal experience. And the gear and benign nature of the scene often lulls rescuers into a complacency. The back up in the water is your experience rather than a shore side rope.

You are your own redundancy.

Surfers make great Swiftwater Technicians. They have already been humbled by waves and know they have to work with the water not against it. Kayakers and rafters brought water knowledge and experience. A command presence does not really help dealing with powerful water. Trying to muscle your way through the challenge tires you fast and saps your chances of survival. The biggest part of training was to engender the idea that entering the water was a last ditch option and if you got in trouble you would need to sort it out yourself, quickly.

Each spring during Swiftwater trainings and assessments it would obvious who were going to be the strongest. They talked less and demonstrated more. I could see their comfort in the water, how they used their body shape to ferry across the current minimizing strokes and preserving their strength. Their heads would stay up and breathing relaxed. When they stopped swimming they accepted the pfd would keep them afloat and would bob low in the eddies without concern.

Trainings quickly sorted people out. It is hard to fake confidence when you have failed to make an eddy and are being pushed out in the current, speeding into the rest of the rapid. People's arms start to flail ineffectively, water-wheeling in place as their legs start to tire and sink. Heads start to swing from side to side and they lose their body position smacking waves with their mouths open and struggling to breath.

From the shore I start to encourage them to look at me, concentrate on breathing and get their body oriented to the flow. On occasion I have to plunge in, riding the rapid with them an arm's length away talking about a self rescue position. Offering a lesson as they start to get control and help themselves. Once I had to grab, and then hold in my arms, a participant as they recovered from a flashback to a childhood near drowning.

I try to train, not haze. Allowing students to find their

comfort point through testing their limits in a controlled setting. Training does not replace experience, it is an adjunct that guides the next stage of development.

ALTHOUGH I AM WHEEZIER and creaky in the joints there is still much to savor in the combination of spring flows and teaching. Feeling the the current whip me off my feet and gasping as the cold bites, my head snaps round to watch the group behind me. Everyone looks good.

Looking downstream at the Sugar Pine Bridge I can see the water pushing off the left wall. The current begins the V out to the center as I cruise along the edge sensing when to roll on my belly, driving into the eddy downstream. Catching it high I spin and crouched in the shallows wave the group in.

Some catch it high, others flap around and miss the turn wallowing in the boil below. Eventually everyone makes it in. A quick debrief and feedback, then a brisk ferry across the river to the Sugar Pine Eddy. Pointing almost upstream with a deliberate stroke and lazy kick I pop into the eddy high, stalling in the flow to grab the riprap.

The group cruise over one at a time. Their position is getting better. People are relaxing, less fighting the current.

Time for another rotation.

17

X MARKS THE SPOT

NOT ALL WHO WANDER ARE LOST, BUT I AM

T he spouse was reluctant to really give much information apart from the fact her husband and son had not made it home after a trip to the park. The location was hard to ascertain but eventually with some coaxing, plus a vehicle description the Badger Pass parking lot was confirmed.

It was winter and the snow was deep. Recent storms had dumped a good amount in the backcountry and it had been cold enough for it to remain soft on top.

The spouse shared a couple of photos and videos as the pair had prepared to head out on their trip. They were up beat and excited in the videos. Their equipment seemed new and their packing disorganized. Physically neither looked like they were ready for the rigors of snowshoeing in deep snow at altitudes above 7000 feet.

The story seemed incomplete to the investigator. Why were they heading out with such urgency, to an undisclosed location did not make sense. There had be more to this.

With more questioning, a kind ear and the right encouragement the spouse cracked. She blurted out they were on a buried treasure hunt. Not the Forrest Fenn quest in the Rockies but a more budget version, lesser know but still potentially lucrative. Hidden in the pages of a novel were clues to solve the location of buried treasure. Her husband had sworn her to secrecy on his mission. He believed he had located the loot in Yosemite.

The investigator kept listening. What clue had he found? And where?

The spouse offered more information. Her husband had been using satellite images of the area to help guide his quest. Scrutinizing the images he had narrowed his search to the area near Badger Pass. Crucially in conducting his search he had ignored the instructions clearly written in the novel preface that the treasure was not buried within a national park boundary.

He felt there been a major breakthrough in his search when he discovered two trees seemingly forming an x on the ground. This could not have happened by chance. Armed with this gem he decided to head out to the spot immediately even though it would be covered by four feet of snow and probably very hard to find. He needed to get there before anyone else.

At this point his son was roped into the mission and they bravely stepped off into the unknown with little experience to hold them back.

With nightfall approaching the ground searchers continued to plug away for clues. The primary area was ringed by a well travelled winter trail pounded down by a multitude of snowshoes and hikers. It offered a firm contrast to the posthole plunging nightmare out in the trees. If the lost party stumbled on it they might recognize it offered salvation.

On the phone with the family giving them an update on

the search the call was interrupted by shouts of joy and garbled message that they had been found. The family had got a cell call from the husband to say they were safe. Sure enough they had stumbled on the trail and a SAR team at the same time. Saved!

Their survival story emerged later and it was a story of ultimately of their misguided resilience in the face of challenge. Almost immediately after they set out one of them had fallen in a creek and got totally wet. This had stalled their plans for the day so they had regrouped. Having spent the night out in the open they had somehow dodged cold injury and welcome the morning eager to continue their search. Their search devolved from looking for treasure to simply searching for a way out of their predicament.

After spending hours trying to figure out where they were they failed to discover their tracks to backtrack. By this time their energy was fading and the idea of another night out would potentially be fatal. On top of that they would never know if the treasure was where they thought it was.

With the shadows lengthening the husband felt he couldn't go on any longer and instructed his son to leave without him. Fortunately this was not pursued as almost immediately after this they were standing on the trail talking to the SAR team looking for them. Fortified with drinks and snacks, on a packed trail with people who knew where they going they were escorted back to their car. Rangers encouraged them to not think about returning in the snow.

The wife called me up to tell me when her family got home she would be laying down the law, no more treasure hunts.

∼

18

BIG SNAKES

This call was for a summer camp student with some sort of impalement injury. Meg and I had answered the request for help and arrived on scene to try to figure out the next step.

There had already been an attempt to locate the crew by one group but the rhododendron had beaten them back. They stood on the road and alternately jabbed their finger at the map and gesticulated at the jungle. We were looking for a better idea of where they had been but the vegetation had scarred them and they were left unable to say much that was useful.

Wrestling in rhododendron forest does that to you. Hours of crawling like a salamander on your belly while you drag your pack changes your view of what is possible. The dense crisscross of branches and unforgivingly steep terrain shrink your world to immediate, normally your next step. The leaves slap you and limbs whip back to smack you without warning. And then you add in leading a group of 15 years on a 3 week Outward Bound course and the true horror emerges. You do get really good at navigation though as it is the only way to reduce your exposure to the night-mare. Suffice it to say that cross-country travel through rhododendron is not for the faint of heart, and the forest had seen fit to flagellate that lesson into the members of the first rescue team.

They were clearly surprised to be approached by a founding member of the Scrawn-arama Wrestling Team, flanked by three smaller, scrawnier women. (Nowadays we would call them all 'wiry'). Their eyebrows went even higher as the county sheriff reached across to the truck hood to shake our hands and say "I'm glad you're here."

The team was polite and made space to give us a better view of the topo map, but it seemed they were concerned about our fitness and safety, understandable given the rhodo-thrashing they had just endured. As we walked away to fine-tune our packs, I heard someone mutter a question to the sheriff, who replied "Naw, it's okay. It's Outward Bound—they ain't human."

We had a grid reference so we knew where they were. And our experience had told us to take the shortest route. A quick drive up the road, a check of the map and we were ready.

This mission would not be just us. We had back up. A crew from the local youth prison would be tagging along to help with the carry out. They were in the area for some forestry work and had been roped in to help. They had coor-dinator/guard. He was not excited about the mission but he had to tag along. He had a machete too.

Meg briefed the crew up. She has a quick wit, fierce intellect and oozes the confidence that says very clearly don't fuck with me. The crew noted this and behaved accordingly. A good start.

Down we plunged, the secret was not to move too quick

and consider each move carefully. Otherwise branches shot up your shorts or snagged on backpack causing discomfort and delay.

Meg struck a straight course down the hill, checking the compass, spotting a tree that looked to be in the right direction and then concentrating on getting to that point before repeating the bearing check. The crew wallowed behind us. They were beginning to get wheezy. Mr Machete brought up the back.

It did not take long on Meg's route to reach the thickness of the creek bottom. As we made our way down, Mr Machete periodically stopped to check his GPS, a relatively new (and somewhat inexact) technology at the time, all the more baffling for not yet having been put into context via mapping bases. He would periodically call Incident Command and relay a string of numbers that bore no correspondence whatsoever to any of the information on the 1953-era USGS topo maps we were using. Fortunately gravity and the magnetosphere remained consistent during the course of our descent, allowing us to arrive at our target destination. A quick scan around and sure enough we spotted the group right where should have been.

We made out way over and checked in with the instructor and then moved to packaging the injured party. She definitely had a significant impalement injury. It was bloody and looked painful. Years later Meg described the injury as "a fucking stump in her knee" and the fact it gave her a case of the sympathetic willies decades later gives testament it its severity. The accompanying medic got some pain meds on board. Once she was in the litter there was some padding around the injury to guard it and then it was time to focus on how to get out.

Meg and I conferenced. The wayback up was too steep

for hauling a litter. Looking down the creek it was a maze of tangled limbs but at least it was moderately flat. Although dauntingly thick with rhododendron. With a good familiarity with the area we knew at the foot of the creek a large open Deer Field was the most likely place we could get vehicle support in.

After some crew coaching on how to carry and pass the litter we moved out.

It was slow and extremely sweaty. The litter caterpillared its way through foliage. The hand line leapfrogged ahead as the litter passed them by. I stayed with the head guarding the patient from being poked in the eye by a vengeful bough.

The amount of purposeful movement around the litter gave the idea good progress had been made. A quick glance back through the thrashed passage and I could see where we had left 15 minutes before. It was going to be a long night.

The machete baring guard had self elected himself to cut a passage through for us. This was not working particularly well. His efforts created a semi path but bordered it with some wicked new spikes to impale ourselves on. He was tiring fast and his cutting strokes were become less frequent. He still checked in with IC to provide updates on the incomprehensible-but-changing-number-stream, which we were able to corroborate by saying "Yes, we're still in the creek."

After half an hour he was done and the litter overtook him. It became safer to concentrate on the litter without the chance of being impaled in the back when he sat down. He started walking behind occasionally swinging at rhododendron that looked at him the wrong way.

The prison crew were getting tired as well. Breaking for

a rest they lit up and began to puff furiously on their cigarettes. Unfortunately this was initially right over the patient so they had to reset in a huddle downwind. The patient remained in remarkable good spirits and was pretty chatty. I think the high flow oxygen probably helped a lot. More pain meds were administered.

This is how it progressed over the next couple of hours. Crawl and drag the litter 100 feet and then stop for a break. Pretty soon all the cigarettes had been smoked. Now the prison just sat quietly breathing hard. Similar to when they had cigarettes but less smokey.

There were frequent radio check ins on the patient and how we were progressing. Patient stable, progress slow. The frequency of radio calls ratcheted up as we got closer to our destination, the Deer Field.

There were more specific requests for where we thought we were. It did not really matter to us as we knew that eventually we would pop out on the Deer Field. But still the calls came.

Finally the shoulders of the creek bank began to slacken, a good indicator we close to the bottom. This detail was conveyed to Incident Command and they respond quickly.

"Litter Team can you see the meadow"

"Negative"

There was a pause, then.

" We are going to fire off some gunshots to help direct you"

I remember looking at Meg and wondering if she had heard the same thing.

Gunshots?

Bang. Bang. Bang. Bang.

Shots in rapid succession. The prison crew started furiously digging down into floor, burying their heads in the leaves. We crouched over the litter.

Meg got on the radio and suggested forcefully that the salvo was not helping and should stop immediately.

It got quiet. Everyone checked in that no one had been wounded. The prison crew were excited, covered in leaves and still wheezy. And not shot.

The gunshot idea had successful scared everyone but in the confusion and with the topography it had been absolutely useless at fixing our exit point. With creek bed opening up moving the litter became more of a walking-upright exercise.

Now we could hear a motor.

A small six-wheeled amphibious vehicle was grinding up the creekbed, bearing two rescue team members. They announced that they were there for the litter, to carry it the remaining 200 yards to the Deer Field. After a few minutes of logistical strategizing, it became clear that in order for the litter to be loaded onto the six-wheeler, at least one (and possibly both) of the current vehicle occupants would have to dismount and follow the vehicle. The patient was in no shape to drive, so the vehicle lumbered back down the creek bed to let IC know that we were near, a report that that we were able to promptly confirm by appearing immediately behind the vehicle, which had a top speed comparable to that of a bunch of tired teenaged inmates who had run out of cigarette

The end was close and with another couple of pushes the Deer Field was gained. And the reason for all the radio calls and gunshots became clear. It was obviously a slow news night in Charlotte as a couple of TV crews were on scene with lights and cameras.

Microphones were thrust in our direction for a soundbite.

"How did the big snakes delay your rescue? How big were they?"

I looked around and wondered what was happening. Snakes? We might have been crawling serpentine for hours but I had not seen or been threatened by a snake during the evacuation.

Meg offered a priceless soundbite " Snakes? I guess there are some out here somewhere...". Gazing at the reporters high heels and listening to them breathlessly report the dangers we had overcome Meg was saddened with the realization that she had ruined one of her best "dress" t-shirts during the rescue.

Being a hero is hard.

Turned out during the waiting game for our appearance a local had been interviewed after a brief foray into the creek bed who had announced the preponderance of large snakes he had seen.

The TV crew did not mention the gunshots.

～

MEG ADDED *in some notes to this story.*

19

CHOICE

Fighting the urge to drive fast I made a mental note that I was not prepared to die in trying to save someone. The appeal for a negotiator had come up short and responding officers had been calling any one with communication skills to help boost resources.

Arriving on scene I wandered over to a couple of rangers in the corner of the parking lot. There was a quiet closure of the immediate area with the drama playing out less than 100 feet unaware visitors continued taking photographs, laughing and shouting.

The initial conversation focused on facts and actions up to that point. A phone call from a spouse had warned about the potential for their partner heading to the area to kill themself. Rangers had arrived on scene just in time to see the individual bail from their vehicle, scurry across the parking lot and over the retaining wall. They took up position on the same rock they had been talked off of two weeks earlier.

Responders had been talking to them for three or four hours by the time I arrived. The responders were positioned

15 feet above them in a small cleared area while they were seated on a rounded edge poised above a thousand foot drop.

Up top the team talked through the plan and details – the spouse and other family members were a couple of hours drive away and dispatch had started identifying potential additional resources to help supplement the negotiating team.

It was a full moon so a steady stream of sightseers continued to drive in and out of the parking lot as the incident continues to play out. Negotiators cycled up and down the slope checking in on possible developments and processing new approaches. Perched on the edge the distraught person was continually looping their conversations, restating over and over again what had brought them to this point. They texted and phoned family to say goodbye – at one point detailing a request for cremation and no memorial. Their stories displayed a high level of paranoia, with themselves painted as a victim of a vast conspiracy.

The family arrived and were drawn off to one side to talk through what was happening. Before the explanation was finished the spouse got a phone call from their partner who instantly requested them at the cliff's edge.

Walking them across the parking lot I talked about de-escalation, leveling emotional reactions and using a measured tone. Accompanied by a ranger they climbed down the access trail and disappeared behind the bushes.

Time passed by – the spouse and sibling swapped positions. Things were not changing at the edge. Up top the family and I went over text messages and reviewed the phone call log.

It was the latest attempt to end their life that month. The previous try had been at the same location two weeks before. Their life had spiraled down after a workplace harassment charge. Despite legal support a suspicious mind saw threats and betrayal everywhere. Off their medications they lost their job and family relationships imploded. That morning their mother had tried to stop them by standing behind their car to stop them leaving. Their father quietly accepted the situation – the brother translated the nuances he might have missed, he added in details and shrugged.

Opening their car we surveyed for keys or a note. A bag was on the backseat, it was searched for clues. Nothing was obvious. The kid seats sat empty and I physically shivered at the thought of how much more complicated this could be.

All this was playing out as a surprising amount of visitors turned into the visa point to look at view under the light of a full moon. Oblivious to the drama playing out next to them they laughed loudly, played lasers over the cliff faces and staged complex flashlight choreography with the rock walls as the backdrop.

The latest visitor arrived then proceeded to comically get trapped in the enormous parking lot right next to the gaggle of ranger vehicles. They struggled for five minutes to complete a three-point turn before driving out of the lot and back onto the main road. As I wandered back across the empty parking lot I laughed out loud as the two cars now trying to park on the eastern end promptly ran into each other. There were no other cars within 100 feet of them and they still managed to have to exchange insurance information.

Hours passed by as a procession of family and negotiators moved up and down the slope. The father and brother slept in the car and I walked back and forth checking the radio and eyeballing the half hidden floodlights below.

By three o'clock they had been sat on the rock for more

than 9 hours. They were getting tired and an attempt to get them to hydrate so much they would have to pee had failed. The team had been looking for the chance to grab them but needed some repositioning to reduce the risk of a rescuer pitching off the edge.

The lead ranger came up and talked through the plan. After hours on the edge they had shifted their position and now a slight opening had been revealed. Coaching had drawn them to a minutely safer spot and they were now within touching distance of family members.

With the right distraction there would be a clear moment to assert control and physically immobilize them. The lead ranger geared up with another rope and a small rack of carabiners, before heading back down the loose trail to the staging area.

I sat in the car waiting for the radio call to say they were going for it. The heater was the only sound. Every once in a while I scanned the parking lot for traffic, the family's car and for any appearances over the perimeter wall.

The radio came alive.

"Negotiations continuing". The responders were going for it. One ranger would appear to lose their balance and start to slip. Hopefully this would be a distraction and the rest of the team could physically jump on the edge sitter before they could react.

Jumping out of the rig I ran to the edge and strained to look down into the shadows. Moments later there was the distinct sound of voices and a cry of pain. Lights stabilized below all directed to one point where I could make out a huddle of bodies. Radios confirmed that the plan had worked and everything was secure below.

Knocking on the car door before I cracked it open the father and brother snapped instantly awake. Reporting out that the decision to end the incident by a direct intervention had been made I told them their family member was safe and would be brought back up.

Rules were laid out – they could watch quietly and approach only with the direction of an officer. I asked them to allow the transfer to play out without distraction. They agreed.

The family stationed themselves back from the edge to watch as the group climbed over the retaining wall. Head-lamps illuminated a slump shouldered figure having their handcuffs checked. An ambulance rolled in and they were quickly moved then secured to the gurney.

Restrained in the back of the ambulance they sat head down and silent. Their spouse chatted with the paramedics about rehydration and possible medications. The father and brother hovered wanting to talk to their relative but were told they were too ashamed to interact at the moment.

After a final check in the ambulance pulled out with the spouse riding along, with the family convoying to a facility that could detain them, help make them safer.

A quick debrief, some tired high fiving and I jumped in my car and headed home. Not going to die for someone. I took the bends slowly and kept my eye out for deer.

20

JUDGEMENT

Suicide.

It is a weighted word in a judgmental world.

Suicides are a quiet fact in the park. People ending their lives in the same place others come to feel life. Callouts can be triggered by distraught family members hoping for a cliffside intervention or a call to dispatch asking for the base of the falls to be cleared to protect others. Law enforcement search for abandoned vehicles or interview witnesses. Notes get forwarded, texts get re-examined. Some people walk off the map, no indicators where they went. Just an inkling that they were in the area with no threads to pursue. Others, drawn to the iconic landscape, end up making a public statement launching from a well travelled viewpoint.

The first suicide I worked forced me to take a long and uncomfortable look at myself. I entered the mission unaware of quite how much unnecessary baggage had been brought along.

And how quickly it needed to be jettisoned.

I had carried the idea of how selfish the act was. How all

the pain had been left with the surviving family. It was an easy blame game with an obvious balancing argument out of the room.

Talking with families a deeper picture emerges that humanizes the tragedy and makes me feel justifiably small for my bias. The stories of accomplishment, tragedy, pain and bad luck paint the more complete portrait of person who chose to end their life.

Whatever reality they were functioning in at the moment they took that step into space, they thought it was best option open to them. The logic that took them to that point possibly thought that the pain, the confusion, the complexity in their lives would finally be gone. It would be the momentary fix that answered a protracted struggle with living.

I discovered I did not need to add to the judgment visited upon them or their families. I just need to respectfully listen to the stories, answer the questions with facts and be kind to those left behind.

Siblings struggle to find the words to tell their parents. Friends frantically call around to piece together the final hours. Shocked workmates realize how little they knew about the person they shared an office with.

In society suicide can shame the victim and then the families. People struggle to find the right words to reopen conversations, skirting the issue and failing to find the easy ground of chit chat. Families withdraw, blaming themselves, possibly struggling to absolve those they love.

Trying to find the right words is not what to focus on. Being present as a kind witness to their pain while sitting in muted support is a good place to start.

Witnessing families coming to terms in the initial stages of loss they predominantly seek opportunities to express themselves to those that can listen. Conversations can be scattered flipping between memories and practicalities. They regularly return to the question that cannot be answered with absolute certainty, why?

Forensically examining the path to their loved one's death drags them through the junctions where intervention might have happened. A recollection of moments becomes a dissection of the past that does not change the present.

Early on there is a created void that cannot be filled. As a responder I have learned that hovering in the wings does not help. You need to present yourself so families have a choice of inviting you in or not. We need to be clear on our role, but actively curate the space for the intimacy of sharing in loss, recognizing grief and nurturing the exchange of memories.

~

IF YOU ARE STRUGGLING with thoughts of suicide or self harm there is help out there. Talk to someone, call a hotline.

It will get better.

There are tools to help coworkers, family and colleagues iden-tify behaviors where professional help can make a difference. Check out the Stress Continuum and the work of the Responder Alliance for more ideas.

~

EPILOGUE

In a small community it is inevitable that you will be touched by death of friends, neighbors and associates. Just living near a wild space magnifies the risks of driving to work or dealing with dangers of a winter storm. If you are connected to those that indulge in high risk adventure activities the chances of that happening are even greater.

It is always unsettling to see these who appear to live a life so actively playing the margin between life and death on a frequent, if not daily, basis to suddenly disappear. One minute they are offering you a s'more, gearing up for an adventure or exchanging a casual goodbye after an evening meal. The next you are hearing radio traffic or getting frantic text chains that are asking you to call immediately.

Small things became the last thing you shared.

These are the moments that haunt you. A phone message you never responded to, an email you delayed answering, a note you failed to send.

Thoughts end up curated round a memory book that

softens with age and fills in the gaps of truth with a rosier picture.

The argument, the falling out, the disagreement over something minor. They might be in there, with a tinge of regret, but I try to keep it positive so the good stuff shines. A recognition that I am not going to be able to mend that fence now.

Twenty four hours after another connected death I found my self roaring at the sky and raging in the woods on my own. In a momentary cell signal window a phone company marketing call makes it through and I end up telling them why I was having a bad day and how they should tightly hug those they love this evening. They did not make a sale but listened and said the right things.

There have been accidents that claimed shiny forces of nature. A simple alignment of circumstances that removed them forever from the physical proximity of those they loved. A terminal cascade of events that rob the future with consistent cruelty.

And it become too many a long time ago.

The sharpest memories of all of them break through the dullness of loss and bring the flicking bright ray of recollection

Laughter, joy, connection.

Remembered campfires, casino nights, deep complex conversations. There were mouse hunts in basecamp cabins, irreverent exchanges, favorite Python sketches, confused drunken foreign language exchanges, surfing secret river waves, beta exchanges as my leg shakes so violently it won't stay on a hold.

I remember storytelling, optimism and generosity. Comfort.

When the call comes to respond I check for the connection. More time leads to more connections.

I do not know how many more I have in me.

AFTERWORD

If you are looking for how to get into Search and Rescue consider checking out some of these links for information, training courses and assessment. If you are frequenting the outdoors consider getting a Wilderness First Aid certificate. Have your adventures that build experiences that build your resiliance. Read up on other's epics and replay yours for lessons, laughs and development.

As Edward Abbey said,

"It is not enough to fight for the land; it is even more important to enjoy it. While you can. While it is still there"

Technical - Swiftwater and Vertical Rescue
    Rescue 3
    Sierra Rescue International
    Rigging for Rescue

Psychological First Aid
    Responder Alliance

First Aid and Wilderness Medicine
   Sierra Rescue International
   Wilderness Medicine Institute (NOLS)
   Wilderness Medical Associates

Organizations
   Mountain Rescue Association
   American Whitewater Association
   Friends of Yosemite Search and Rescue

Published Materials
   Mountaineering: Freedom of the Hills - The Mountaineers
   Accidents in American Mountaineering - American Alpine Club
   Whitewater and River Rescue Field Guide - Munger

ABOUT THE AUTHOR

Moose Mutlow has been professionally involved in education and the outdoors for more than 30 years. Moose's first job when he left high school was as a water bailiff on a river north of Birmingham, England. He swapped those cold mornings to be a canoe instructor in the Ardeche, managed a beach concession on the Mediterranean, an Outward Bound instructor in Australia, he taught High School science in the Kalahari Desert, and been a classroom teacher, education director, elite Sport Academy Principal, and is currently the Senior Project Director for Nature-Bridge. He has worked in a zoo, been a bar manager, volunteered as a social worker, and was a poorly rewarded street performer on too many occasions. He has been on expeditions in Southern Africa and the Arctic. He spent a couple of weeks at the Denali Basecamp on a SAR patrol and realized he really was not that keen on mountaineering.

At some point he went to college and got an Honors Degree in Environmental Science and a Post Graduate High School Teaching Certificate in Biology and Physical Education.

Moose is a Rescue 3 Agency Instructor and has been the Senior Swift-water Instructor for Yosemite Search and Rescue for more than a decade. He has been featured on NPR and regional/national news discussing water safety and accident prevention. He was the only person shown crying in the YOSAR documentary – Dangerous Season.

Moose developed and has instructed the Family Liaison Officer training in Yosemite National Park since 2010. Moose has been nationally recognized for his work as a Lead FLO and has trained the FLO's in Yosemite, Grand Teton, Yellowstone, Arches and Smoky Mountain National Parks.

He spent 12 years as an Outward Bound instructor in Australia, USA and Wales. For five years Moose managed the Instructor Development Programs at North Carolina Outward Bound School. Alongside instructional development Moose has instructed Vietnam Veterans, worked with addicts in recovery, mixed ability programming, corporate executives, and adolescents. Moose graduated from the first NOLS Professional River Instructor program and trained with Rigging for Rescue in high angle rescue. After more than 2000 instructional days in the field he does not miss thrashing around in rhododendrons with a 70lb backpack in the middle of a thunderstorm.

Moose helped develop Yosemite National Parks "Red Bear, Dead Bear" program to reduce wildlife road-kill. After receiving a series of richly deserved speeding tickets in the park he conducted an 18-month informal study and presented his findings to the scientific community in the park. The presentation, entitled "Splat goes the Weasel", helped identify the issues of concentrated road-kill locations and introduced the idea of roadside signage to encourage motorists to stick to posted speed limits. Moose has subsequently not received any more moving violations in the park.

Moose has worked in First Response, SAR and emergency services for more than two decades as a SAR technician, W-EMT, Ski Patroller and Senior Trainer.

He failed his cycling proficiency test aged 10 – it was easily the worst student experience of his life. He references that needlessly humiliating morning to this day to try and make all instructional experiences positive and supportive. He eventually passed the proficiency test aged 11.

Moose is available for contract trainings, advice, public speaking and consulting.

Website – www.moosemutlow.com

ALSO BY MOOSE MUTLOW

When Accidents Happen

Managing Crisis Communication as a Family Liaison Officer

ASIN : B08GSTiFFY

I wrote this book to hopefully broaden the resources available to FLOs to draw from and reference during an assignment. Being a FLO can be a brutal learning experience with so much being learned on the job. I wanted to present some of the lessons that I learned to better prepare others to be successful in the job. Writing took considerably longer than I thought it would. I ended up replaying incidents and reflecting more deeply on the experience. It was painful at first, then cathartic. I did not realize the depth of emotional baggage I was carrying as a witness to some many others profound loss. I have more clarity in what I could do better and a clearer understanding of the role after writing this book. Ultimately I hope the text will be a living thing that others adapt for their own programs and needs. It is definitely one way of tackling the complexities of the role - it is not the only way.

Made in the USA
Monee, IL
02 July 2022